Jokes and the Unconscious

by Daphne Gottlieb
and Diane DiMassa

CLEIS
PRESS

Published in the United States by Cleis Press Inc.,
P.O. Box 14697, San Francisco, California 94114.

Printed in the United States.
Cover design: Scott Idleman
Cover Art: Diane DiMassa
Cleis Press logo art: Juana Alicia
First Edition.
10 9 8 7 6 5 4 3 2 1

This is a work of fiction. Any and all resemblances to real
persons, living or dead, are entirely coincidental.

Acknowledgments

Daphne and Diane would like to thank Kate Black and Ben Cave, whose timely and generous loan of technology made this book possible. Daphne would also like to thank Danielle and Jonathan, for knowing lots of jokes. Diane would additionally like to thank Black Ink and White Out.

"The idea of comic relief has been present in everything from the Greek theatre to Shakespeare, and we all understand that laughter is a great way to release pent-up emotions. This same phenomenon is the origin of 'off color' or 'tasteless' jokes – laughter mediates between us and our discomfort with mortality, sexuality, ethnicity or any other touchy subject."

– Sigmund Freud, *Jokes and Their Relation to the Unconscious*

A JOKE I KNOW

Three soldiers lose their way in the jungle and are captured by hostile soldiers. They are brought before the leader of the other army, who tells them that they are now prisoners of war. But because high-ranking officials cannot decide what to do with the soldiers, the prisoners will be allowed to choose one of two fates. General Mort looks at the three men and thrusts a finger in the air.

"Will you have Death," he asks them, "or Infilt?"
"Infilt?" the men ask. "What is 'Infilt'?"
It is explained that Infilt entails being sodomized by every male in the army, an Army known far and wide for its numbers.
The first man has heard enough. "Death!" he says.
"Death!" exclaims General Mort, nodding sagely. The man is thrown over the cliff to the alligators.
The second man has also heard enough. "Death!" he cries.
"Death!" exclaims General Mort, nodding sagely. The man is thrown over the cliff to the alligators.
The third man is frightened. He shudders and swallows. He says nothing.
"Well?!" thunders General Mort.
The man shudders and swallows. Finally, he whispers, "Infilt."
General Mort thrusts his arm in the air. "Death by Infilt!" he booms.

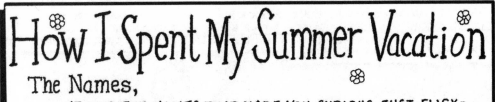

How I Spent My Summer Vacation

The Names,

IT WAS THE NAMES THAT MADE YOU CURIOUS. JUST FLICK-ERING THOUGHTS, IMAGINING WHERE THADDEUS FISHTON LIVED, WHAT MURRAY HELLWIG III DID FOR A LIVING, AND WHAT POOR HARRY KARRY'S PARENTS WERE THINKING WHEN THEY NAMED HIM. THE NAME WAS, OF COURSE, THE FIRST THING YOU'D SEE.

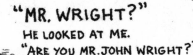

"MR. WRIGHT?"
HE LOOKED AT ME.
"ARE YOU MR. JOHN WRIGHT?"

THE OXYGEN TUBES BOBBED LIGHTLY, THE PLASTIC CRAB CLIPPED TO HIS NOSE.

I TOOK A *DEEP BREATH*

GOOD MORNING, MR. WRIGHT. I'M FROM THE HOSPITAL BUSINESS OFFICE DOWNSTAIRS. WHEN YOU WERE ADMITTED YESTERDAY WE NEVER GOT YOUR SIGNATURE ON THIS FORM — NOW THE FIRST SIGNATURE WE NEED IN ORDER TO BILL YOUR INSURANCE COMPANY DIRECTLY AND THE SECOND SIGNATURE ALLOWS THE HOSPITAL TO RELEASE YOUR HOSPITAL RECORDS TO THE INSURANCE COMPANY SO THAT THEY KNOW WHAT THEY'RE PAYING FOR — OKAY —

CAN YOU SIGN THIS FOR ME?

HIS HEAD HAD BEEN SHAVED AND BLUE MARKER PEN GRAFFITIED HIS HAIRLINE IN A JAGGED SCRAWL. THE TUBES SWAYED A LITTLE BIT AS HE STRUGGLED TO SIT A BIT MORE UPRIGHT. "WHA?" HE SAID, BLINKING AT ME, FISH-EYED. THE SHORT GOWN BRUSHED FURTHER UP, A TENT ON HIS THIGHS.

"WANDA WANTED ME TO MENTION TO YOU THAT THERE MAY BE TIMES WHEN YOU WALK INTO A ROOM THAT A MAN MAY BE, WELL, HIS MEMBER MAY BE EXPOSED. ACT AS NATURAL AS YOU CAN. MOST OF THEM DON'T DO IT ON PURPOSE. IN FACT, MOST OF THE TIME THEY DON'T EVEN KNOW. SO JUST DON'T PANIC. WITH THE PATIENTS FROM THE GROUP HOMES, SOMETIMES IT'S BETTER TO ASK AT THE DESK IF SOMEONE COULD GO IN AND COVER THEM UP.

I'M FROM THE BUSINESS OFFICE, MR. WRIGHT, AND I NEED YOUR SIGNATURE ON THIS FORM. CAN YOU HELP ME?

SOMEBODY HELP ME

HE LOOKED UP AT ME, AND I WAS LOOKING AT THE BLUE SCRAWL ON HIS HEAD THROB LIKE A BABY'S WHEN THE PLATES HAVEN'T FUSED TOGETHER YET SO YOU CAN SEE THEIR PULSE BEAT.

THE NURSE BRISTLED BY ME LIKE A CAT. STROKING THE OXYGEN TUBES LIKE WHISKERS, SHE PEERED INTO HIS EYES. SHE WAS BRISK WHITE STARCH.

GOOD MORNING, MR. WRIGHT. DO YOU KNOW WHERE YOU ARE?

S-S-S-SYRACUSE

"YES, THAT'S VERY GOOD. I'LL BE BACK IN A MINUTE." SHE STOOD UP AND STARED AT ME HARD, SEALING HER LIPS TOGETHER.

I TURNED TO LEAVE AND I THINK SHE NODDED AT ME.

THERE ARE SOME THINGS YOU JUST CAN'T TELL PEOPLE ABOUT. IT'S NOT NECESSARILY THAT THEY MEAN TOO MUCH TO EXPRESS. IT'S JUST THAT THERE'S NOT NECESSARILY MUCH OF A POINT IN THE TELLING; LITTLE THINGS THAT HAVE HAD TREMENDOUS IMPACT ARE MAUDLIN AND SOUND CONTRIVED IN THE RETELLING.

MY WATCH STOPPED THE DAY MY FATHER DIED. THAT'S TOO CLUMSY TO WRITE ABOUT WITH ANY GRACE. WATCH: STOPPED = FATHER: DEAD. THE SYMBOLS ARE TOO EAGER, THE EQUATION TOO READY, SOMETHING HIGH SCHOOL POETS WOULD USE.

I KILL WATCHES ALL THE TIME. SOMETHING ABOUT MY BODY MAGNETISM, I'M TOLD. I'VE GONE THROUGH THREE BATTERIES SO FAR THIS YEAR.

MECHANICAL APPLIANCES COME WITH NO WARRANTIES PROTECTING AGAINST ACCIDENTAL IRONIES, AGAINST WATCHES THAT KEEP SUGGESTIVE TIME, RECORDERS THAT WARP VOICES, PICTURES THAT PRESERVE WRONG GLANCES AND PAINED EXPRESSIONS, PICTURES THAT ARE HAZY AND OBSCURE. TELEVISIONS THAT DEPICT LUXURY, YOUTH, FAME, FORTUNE. EVERY MOVIE HAS A DEATH SCENE. ALL BETRAY.

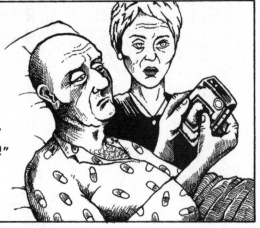

MY FATHER, FROM HIS BED, HIS FINAL DAY, ASKS FOR HIS DICTAPHONE. HE IS ABSOLUTEY DETERMINED – HE HAS TO WORK, HE'S PANICKED – HE HAS TO GET THIS ALL DOWN, TAKE A FEW MORE NOTES THAT MIGHT BE USEFUL SOMEDAY. HIS MORPHINE-THICK SPEECH IS GARBLED, BUT THE ANTI-PSYCHOTICS SEEM TO BE WORKING. HE IS NO LONGER MUMBLING TO MY MOTHER THAT THE KING AND QUEEN OF *CZECHOSLOVAKIA* ARE COMING AND TO "SEAT THEM RIGHT HERE!" HE THUMPS HIS PILLOW, THEN POINTS A FINGER IN THE AIR.

"AND. I WOULD LIKE SOME CHOCOLATE MILK."

HE MOANS INTO THE CONDENSED MICROPHONE.

HE STOPS THE TAPE.

HE MOANS INTO THE CONDENSED MICROPHONE.

HE STOPS THE TAPE.

HE MOANS INTO THE CONDENSED MICROPHONE.

HE STOPS THE TAPE.

DAYS OR WEEKS OR MONTHS LATER I PLAY THE TAPE, WANTING MY FATHER BACK, WANTING MY FATHER TO RISE FROM THE TAPE.

I LISTEN THROUGH FROM THE BEGINNING OF THE TAPE, WITH INTERN RECOMMENDATIONS, PROTOCOL EVALUATIONS, CORRESPONDENCES, AS THE TAPE REPLAYS DAYS, WEEKS, MONTHS,

AND THEN MOANS.

The T-cells the t-cells the c-, the see, the sea...
Thus offsetting some inevitable event, I speed death...
Got to... (the voice slows to underwater, the batteries)

...got to find those cells.

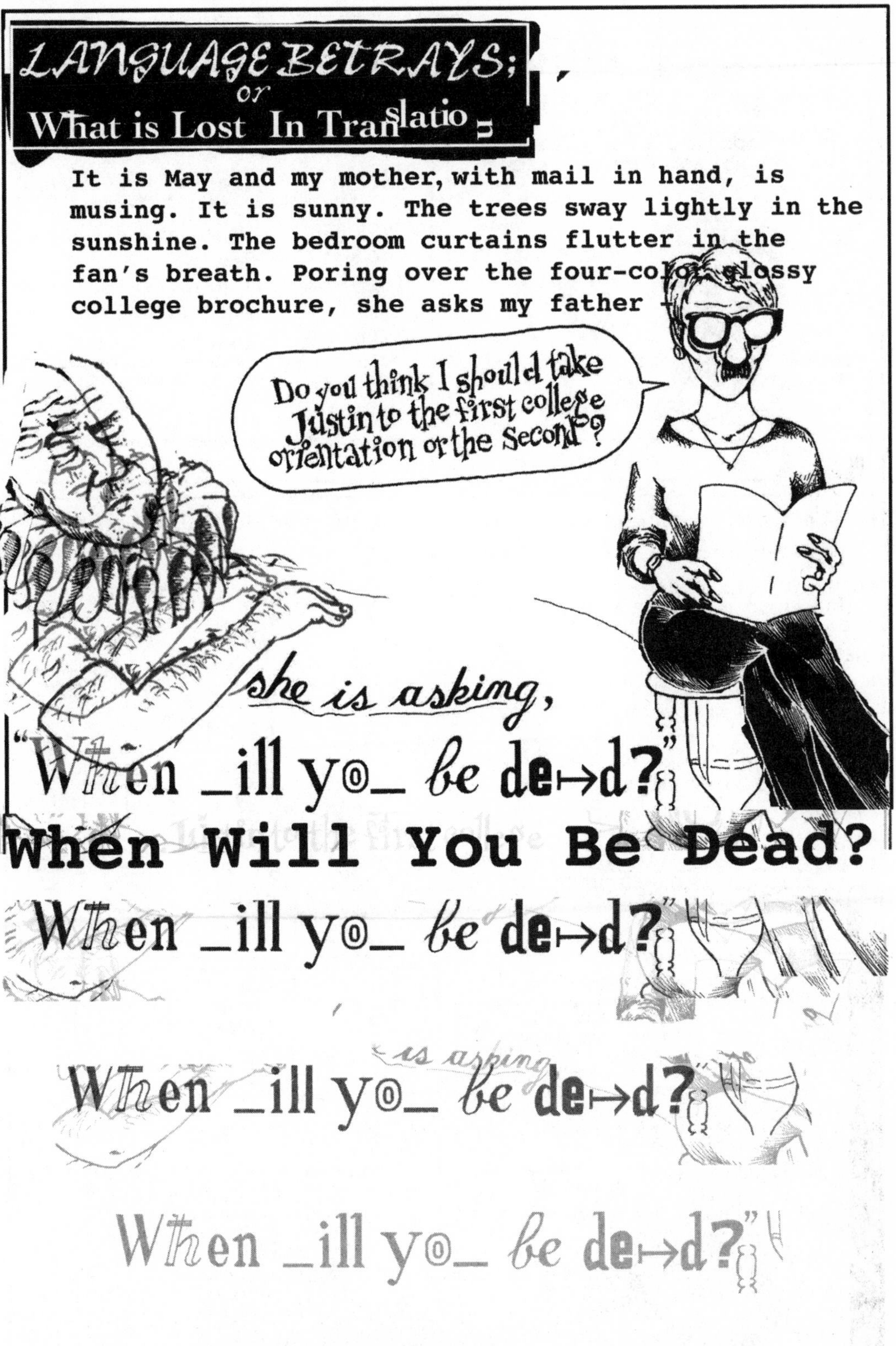

It is May and my mother, with mail in hand, is musing. It is sunny. The trees sway lightly in the sunshine. The bedroom curtains flutter in the fan's breath. Poring over the four-color glossy college brochure, she asks my father –

> Do you think I should take Justin to the first college orientation or the second?

she is asking,

"When _ill yo_ be de→d?"

When Will You Be Dead?

When _ill yo_ be de→d?

When _ill yo_ be de→d? *is asking*

When _ill yo_ be de→d?"

When Will You Be Dead?

TYPE 0

IS THE CODE WE USE FOR ADMISSIONS THAT ARE NOT ACCIDENT RELATED.

TYPE ONE IS THE CODE FOR A MOTOR VEHICLE ACCIDENT.

TYPE TWO IS A JOB-RELATED INJURY COVERED BY COMPENSATION.

TYPE THREE IS AN INJURY SUSTAINED IN AN ASSAULT.

TYPE FOUR IS AN INJURY IN THE WORK-PLACE NOT COVERED BY COMPENSATION.

TYPE FIVE IS A MOTOR VEHICLE ACCIDENT SUSTAINED ON A MOTORCYCLE OR WHILE A CRIME WAS IN PROGRESS.

TYPE SIX IS ACCIDENT-RELATED INJURY/OTHER

THE ADMITTING DESK MAKES MISTAKES ON THEIR FORMS ALL THE TIME.

WHEN WE FIND ONE, WE ARE SUPPOSED TO

1. MAKE A PRINT OF THE ERROR
2. CIRCLE IT IN RED
3. CORRECT THE ERROR ON THE COMPUTER
4. MAKE A NEW PRINT
5. LABEL THE CORRECTED COPY
6. FILL OUT AN ERROR DESCRIPTION FORM

7. AND SEND IT ALL OVER TO BILLING THROUGH INTER-OFFICE MAIL.

I USED TO THINK IT WAS INTER-OFFICE MAIL, BUT THE BAG IS CLEARLY LABELED "INTRA."

MARILYN HAMMOND IS IN AND OUT OF THE SIXTH FLOOR SOMETIMES TWO AND THREE TIMES A WEEK. ADMITTING HAS THE ACCIDENT CODE ON HER FORM AS TYPE SIX.

THE CODE FOR BREAST CANCER IS SUPPOSED TO BE ZERO. I DO NOT CHANGE IT.

NOBODY HAS BOTH BREASTS AMPUTATED ON PURPOSE.

OOPS!!

the Serpent and the Apple

IT IS THREE-THIRTY IN THE AFTERNOON OF MY FIRST DAY AT WORK AT THE HOSPITAL - LAST SUMMER, I WORKED AT A DELI, MAKING CUCUMBER-AND-HAVARTI SANDWICHES FOR YUPPIES.

GIVE ME A...

... VASECTOMY?

Co

TIP US YOU CHE FUC

YOU NEED THIS BUY

WHEN MY FATHER WAS DYING, HE ASKED A FRIEND IN HUMAN RESOURCES TO MAKE SURE I HAD A SUMMER JOB.

I CAN GET MY OWN JOB.

THIS ONE'S BETTER.

I KNEW BETTER THAN TO ARGUE.

IT'S MY FIRST DAY AT THE HOSPITAL AND EVERYTHING SMELLS LIKE RUBBING ALCOHOL, FLOOR CLEANER, AND SHIT.

GOODNIGHT. SEE YOU TOMORROW.

LOUISE IS PUTTING HER COMB, HER LIPSTICK, AND HER AVON CATALOG IN HER PURSE. SHE LOOKS TIRED, BABBLING ABOUT HER STEPDAUGHTER'S DANCE RECITAL, AND THE COSTUME THAT COST SEVENTY-FIVE DOLLARS, AND HER PRESCRIPTION ANTIDEPRESSANTS. LOUISE WORKS SEVEN-THIRTY TO THREE-THIRTY, AND A FEW HOURS ON SUNDAYS. JUDY IS IN A MEETING AND MELANIE IS OUT ON THE FLOOR, ASSISTING PEOPLE WHO WISH TO APPLY FOR MEDICAID. I AM ALONE IN THE OFFICE, BORED AND FRIGHTENED THAT THE PHONE WILL RING AND SOMEONE WILL ASK ME A QUESTION THAT I CANNOT ANSWER.

9

I'M NOT EVEN SURE I KNOW HOW TO ANSWER THE PHONE PROPERLY HERE

DON'T YOU FUCKING EVEN DARE

WE ARE PART OF THE

BUSINESS OFFICE CALLED THE PRELIMINARY BILLING GROUP AND THE SIGN ABOVE OUR DOOR SAYS

DISCHARGE

AND THE PICTURE I.D. CARD IS LABELED

CONTROLLER'S OFFICE →

I OPEN MY DESK DRAWER AND FONDLE MY PAPER CLIPS, THE RED PENS FOR MARKING FINANCIAL CODES ON FOLDERS, MY STAMP PAD AND DATE STAMP. I AM BORED.

CLEK CLEK CLEK CLEK

I DO THE ONE THING I KNOW HOW TO DO; I TYPE IN MY NAME AND SEE MY MEDICAL RECORDS APPEAR ON THE SCREEN

TIKKATA TIKKATA TICKA TICKA TIK TIK TIC

EVIDENCE OF MY WISDOM TEETH EXTRACTION AND MONONUCLEOSIS TESTS. PRESSING A BUTTON, I SEE MY INSURANCE INFORMATION.

I MAKE A PRINT OF THIS.

GO, ASHA GO!

MM BIK BIK MM BIKBIK MM BIK MM BIK

I type my father's name into the computer, witnessing the dates of his heart attack, his leg embolism, his chemotherapy treatments. There is no "EXP" in flashing letters by his name, no documentation of his death. I do not know why. I pull up my sister's, brother's, and mother's records.

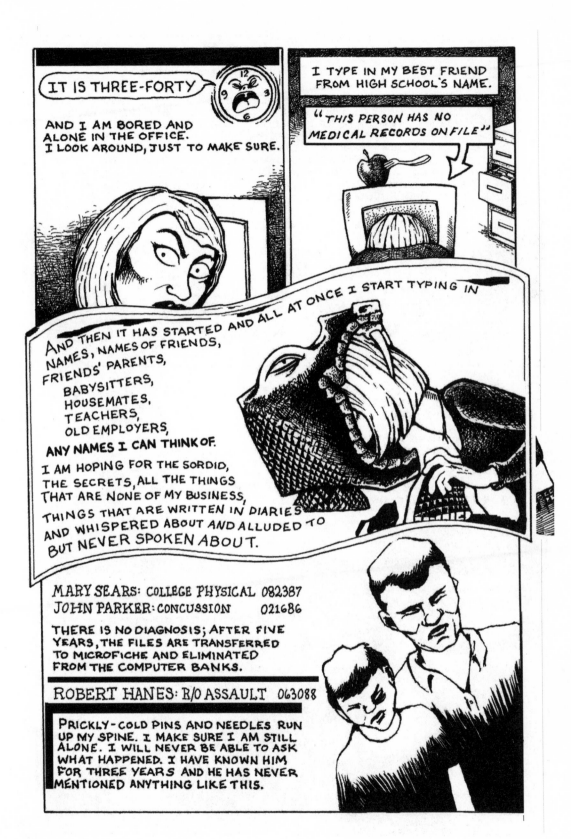

IT IS THREE-FORTY

AND I AM BORED AND ALONE IN THE OFFICE. I LOOK AROUND, JUST TO MAKE SURE.

I TYPE IN MY BEST FRIEND FROM HIGH SCHOOL'S NAME.

"THIS PERSON HAS NO MEDICAL RECORDS ON FILE"

AND THEN IT HAS STARTED AND ALL AT ONCE I START TYPING IN NAMES, NAMES OF FRIENDS, FRIENDS' PARENTS, BABYSITTERS, HOUSEMATES, TEACHERS, OLD EMPLOYERS, ANY NAMES I CAN THINK OF.

I AM HOPING FOR THE SORDID, THE SECRETS, ALL THE THINGS THAT ARE NONE OF MY BUSINESS, THINGS THAT ARE WRITTEN IN DIARIES AND WHISPERED ABOUT AND ALLUDED TO BUT NEVER SPOKEN ABOUT.

MARY SEARS: COLLEGE PHYSICAL 082387
JOHN PARKER: CONCUSSION 021686

THERE IS NO DIAGNOSIS; AFTER FIVE YEARS, THE FILES ARE TRANSFERRED TO MICROFICHE AND ELIMINATED FROM THE COMPUTER BANKS.

ROBERT HANES: R/O ASSAULT 063088

PRICKLY-COLD PINS AND NEEDLES RUN UP MY SPINE. I MAKE SURE I AM STILL ALONE. I WILL NEVER BE ABLE TO ASK WHAT HAPPENED. I HAVE KNOWN HIM FOR THREE YEARS AND HE HAS NEVER MENTIONED ANYTHING LIKE THIS.

IT IS FOUR-TWENTY

Enough time for a few more names.

I remember a boy I used to go to the movies with once in a while, a few years ago before he left for college in Pennsylvania. I know he has a heart condition. I pull up his file and find he was hospitalized in May. I go two screens further and see his address, phone number, and current employer. Faster than the phone book that would have given me no inkling that he was in town, only a phone listing under his mother's name. I make a print and stick it in my purse, folded.

I put in the name of a man I was madly in love with for two years. We had everything all planned out. He would be in a band and I would work for a magazine and we would live in New York City and we would have two children, two cats and a dog, and not eat red meat. Then we broke up. Now he has a new, ugly, teenage girlfriend. She wears braces. I tell everyone that I hope they are happy. Mostly I hope that he cuts his lips on her braces.

THEODORE BECK: PENILE WARTS   061188

FOUR-THIRTY.
I make a print, put it in my purse, and smile to myself while I put my lipstick, my I.D. card, and my hairspray in my purse.

12

SPOONFUL OF SUGAR

A man goes to see his doctor, since he has a terrible case of tennis elbow. Without as much as asking him to roll up his sleeve, the doctor insists he pee in a cup. "What does that have to do with my elbow?!?" asks the perplexed man. "You'll see," says the doctor. The man does as he is asked, and soon, the doctor is pouring the urine sample into a machine in the examining room. The machine spits a print out to the doctor.

"Let's see," says the doctor. "Your cholesterol is a little high, and you have a slight heart murmur that you've had since you were a child."

"That's amazing," says the man, "but—"

"As far as your elbow goes, you've got tennis elbow. Stay off the courts for a couple of weeks and you'll be fine."

"The machine can tell all that from my urine sample?"

"Yes," says the doctor. "Technology is an amazing thing. Now, stay off the courts and come back and see me in a couple of weeks."

The man does as his doctor asks, but he can't help himself. He's stymied by the machine. So before he sees his doctor again, he grabs some of the water from the toilet in his son's bathroom, a few strands of hair from his daughter's hairbrush, a spoonful of the dog's shit from the yard and, for good measure, stirs his urine into the mix with his wife's coffee spoon.

He brings the cup to his unsuspecting doctor who calmly pours the foul cocktail into the machine.

"Hmm," says the doctor.

"Technology not working so well, doc?" asks the man.

"Let me put it this way," says the doctor. "Your son is gay. Please have him see a supportive therapist as soon as possible. Your dog has worms and needs to see the vet. Your wife is pregnant with twins and you're not the father, and—" the doctor says, pulling his glasses down on his nose, "if you don't stop jacking off all day, that tennis elbow is never going to get better."

Ways To Leave

MY FATHER IS SLEEPING, FINGERS SOFTLY CURVED AT HIS SIDES.
I SIT CURLED UP IN A BLANKET ON THE FLOOR. IT IS MONTHS SINCE HE
STOPPED ASKING, "IS IT HOT IN HERE OR IS IT JUST ME?"
HE KNOWS IT IS JUST HIM, AND SO ON A SUNNY DAY IN THE MIDDLE OF MAY,
HE LIES ON TOP OF HIS COVERS IN HIS BOXER SHORTS, HIS DISTENDED
STOMACH BARE WHERE THE TEE SHIRT HAS BEEN PULLED UP.
TWO LARGE FANS BLOW HIM COOL AND I AM CHILLED BENEATH MY BLANKET,
SWEATPANTS, SOCKS AND SWEATER.

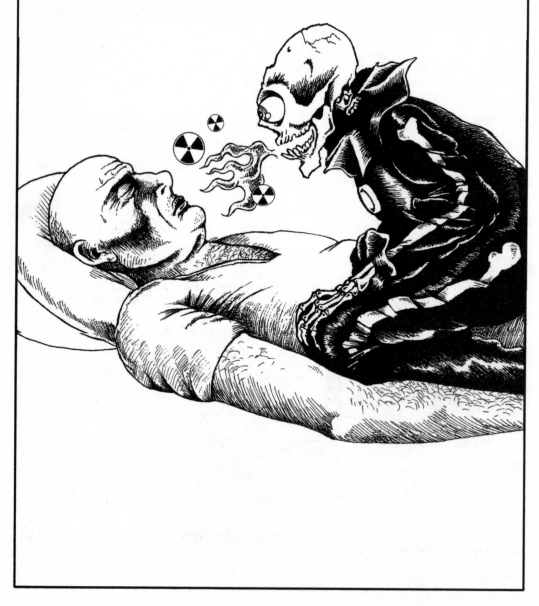

HE ONLY LEAVES FOR THE BATHROOM.

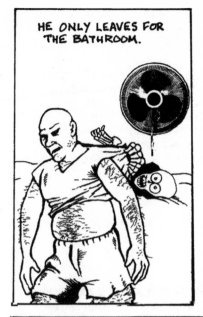

HE AWAKENS, MUMBLES SOMETHING TO MY MOTHER, WHO BRUSHES HER HAND OVER HIS COOL FOREHEAD, NODDING. SHE HANDS HIM HIS ICE WATER WITH THE FLEX-O-STRAW AND LOOKS DOWN AT ME.

WHAT DID HE SAY?

"YOUR FATHER HAS A RECURRING DREAM THAT HE IS SWIMMING." MY FATHER NODS. "SWIMMING"

BEFORE THE NEIGHBORHOOD POOL COLLAPSED AND HAD TO BE FILLED IN AND BECAME A GARDEN, MY FATHER WOULD SWIM ON HOT SUMMER DAYS AFTER WORK.

THE MOST POWERFUL THING I'D EVER SEEN, THE HEAVY MAN WHO LUMBERED A BIT ON LAND, CUTTING CLEANLY THROUGH THE WATER, BEATING ME AT RACES, LITTLE BEADS OF WET CLINGING LIKE STICKY PEARLS TO THE GRAY CURLING HAIR ON THE TOPS OF HIS SHOULDERS.

SOMETIMES HE WOULD JUST FLOAT ON THE INFLATABLE RAFT, EYES CLOSED, FEET DANGLING.

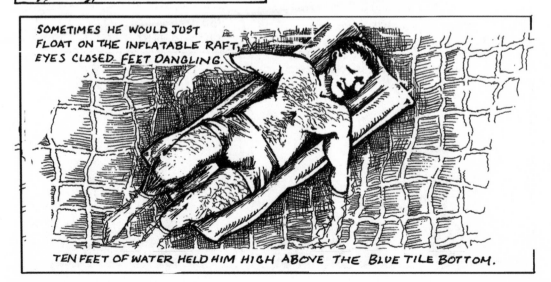

TEN FEET OF WATER HELD HIM HIGH ABOVE THE BLUE TILE BOTTOM.

HOSPITAL MORNINGS ARE BUSY.

DATE-STAMPING THE DRG FORMS, PROCESSING THE FOLDERS FROM THE NIGHT BEFORE, GOING OUT ON THE FLOOR TO OBTAIN SIGNATURES. THE EARLY AFTERNOONS ARE BUSY, TOO, GOING THROUGH INPATIENT FILES AND PREPARING AND DELIVERING COURTESY DISCHARGE CARDS TO PATIENTS WHOSE INSURANCE HAS BEEN VERIFIED.

I AM NEW AND I MAKE MISTAKES.

SEE THE GUARDS IN BLUE? THAT PATIENT WAS SENT TO US FROM A CORRECTIONAL FACILITY.

DID YOU NOTICE THE SCENE IN THAT ROOM? LET'S WALK BY AGAIN AND LOOK IN.

"MOST OF THEM ARE AIDS PATIENTS. THEIR BUSINESS OFFICE DEALS DIRECTLY WITH OURS. IF YOU NEED ANYTHING FROM THEM FOR ANY REASON, DEAL WITH THE GUARDS."

WHITE

"YOU HAVE NO BUSINESS WITH THESE PATIENTS."

Louise tells me this
Too Late

I SEE THE GUARD AT THE DOOR AND HE IS VERY FRIENDLY, TIPPING HIS HAT.

"GOOD MORNING, MISS."

ENTERING THE ROOM, I ANNOUNCE TO SALVADOR DIEGO THAT THE HOSPITAL HAS ALL THE INSURANCE INFORMATION NECESSARY, AND WHEN THE DOCTORS SAY HE MAY LEAVE, HE IS FREE TO GO. IT IS NOT MANDATORY THAT HE STOP AT THE DISCHARGE OFFICE. HE MAY BE WHEELED OUT DIRECTLY.

SALVADOR WOULD LOOK LIKE A VERY THIN MAN WITH VERY SAD EYES, EXCEPT WITH ALL THE TUBES COMING OUT OF HIM, HE SORT OF RESEMBLES A SEA CREATURE. SALVADOR DOES NOT SPEAK ENGLISH. SALVADOR MAY NOT BE ALIVE FOR HIS DISCHARGE.

SALVADOR LOOKS CONFUSED AND SAYS NOTHING, THE SAD EYES UNFOCUSED ON THE WALL.

THE GUARD IS BITING HIS LIP TO KEEP FROM LAUGHING. HE KNOWS THAT I AM NEW, THAT INMATES DO NOT RECEIVE COURTESY.

I UNFOCUS MY EYES AND STARE AT THE WALL

I TELL LOUISE AND LOUISE LAUGHS AND TELLS WANDA THE DRAGON LADY WHO HAS STOPPED BY TO SEE HOW I AM DOING IN MY NEW JOB, IF I AM HAVING ANY PROBLEMS.
WANDA THE DRAGON LADY SPITS A HARSH CHUCKLE, PURSES HER LIPS,
"THAT'S VERY FUNNY. AN ACCIDENT IS AN ACCIDENT. JUST DON'T MAKE A PRACTICE OF IT."

LOUISE TELLS ME THAT SHE WAS GIVEN THIS JOB BECAUSE SHE DOES NOT MIND FIRING PEOPLE.

I BEAR THIS IN MIND.

STOP!

That Joke
Isnt Funny

ANYMORE

IT IS THREE-THIRTY AND I AM BORED AND ALONE IN THE OFFICE AND MY GAME OF PULLING NAMES UP FROM THE COMPUTER HAS BEEN NEARLY EXHAUSTED.

I HAVE RUN OUT OF NAMES FROM THE PRESENT AND IT HAS BECOME A GAME OF "WHATEVER HAPPENED TO," AS I POP IN THE NAMES OF PEOPLE I HAVE NOT SPOKEN TO IN YEARS.

TWO OF MY NURSERY SCHOOL PLAY-MATES HAVE NO MEDICAL RECORDS. THE DOCTOR WHO GAVE ME MY I.Q. TEST WHEN I WAS FIVE, SHOWING ME MATRICES AND PLAYING GAMES, WAS IN A CAR ACCIDENT THREE YEARS AGO.

THE BOYS WOULD NOT LET ME PLAY WITH THE BLOCKS THAT LOOK LIKE BRICKS WITH THEM BECAUSE I AM A GIRL, AND SO HESTER AND I QUIETLY PLAY WITH OUR STUFFED ANIMALS IN THE CORNER.

HEY! I MAY BE FIVE, BUT I ALREADY HAVE A HIGHLY DEVELOPED GRASP OF GENDER POLARIZATION, SO FUCK OFF FROM THEM BRICKS!!

YEAH! WHAT PART OF "WEE-WEE" DON'T YOU UNDERSTAND?? JESUS!

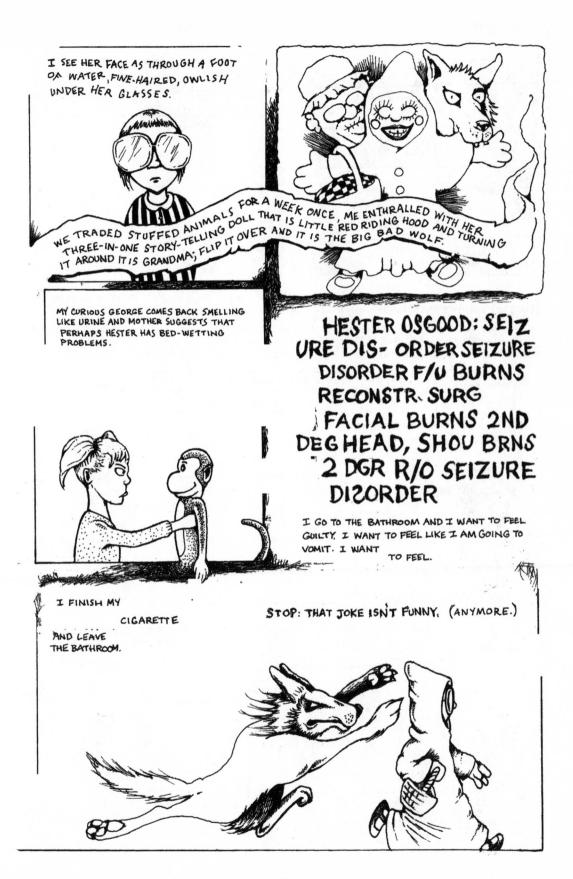

I SEE HER FACE AS THROUGH A FOOT OF WATER, FINE-HAIRED, OWLISH UNDER HER GLASSES.

WE TRADED STUFFED ANIMALS FOR A WEEK ONCE, ME ENTHRALLED WITH HER THREE-IN-ONE STORY-TELLING DOLL THAT IS LITTLE RED RIDING HOOD AND TURNING IT AROUND IT IS GRANDMA; FLIP IT OVER AND IT IS THE BIG BAD WOLF.

MY CURIOUS GEORGE COMES BACK SMELLING LIKE URINE AND MOTHER SUGGESTS THAT PERHAPS HESTER HAS BED-WETTING PROBLEMS.

HESTER OSGOOD: SEIZURE DIS- ORDER SEIZURE DISORDER F/U BURNS RECONSTR. SURG FACIAL BURNS 2ND DEG HEAD, SHOU BRNS 2 DGR R/O SEIZURE DISORDER

I GO TO THE BATHROOM AND I WANT TO FEEL GUILTY. I WANT TO FEEL LIKE I AM GOING TO VOMIT. I WANT TO FEEL.

I FINISH MY CIGARETTE AND LEAVE THE BATHROOM.

STOP: THAT JOKE ISN'T FUNNY. (ANYMORE.)

CAN YOU HANDLE SOMETHING DIFFICULT?

"WHAT DO YOU MEAN 'DIFFICULT?'" "CHECK THIS OUT," SAYS LOUISE, HER SILVER-SPANGLED TEE SHIRT SPARKLING UNDER THE FLUORESCENT LIGHTS.

RITA TADROS: TYLENOL INGESTION 071189

"THEY HAVE INSURANCE WHICH WILL COVER HER, SINCE SHE'S A FULL-TIME STUDENT, BUT HERE'S THE RUB: THE INSURANCE ONLY WORKS IF INGESTION WAS ACCIDENTAL. SHE TOOK FORTY TYLENOL. WE DON'T THINK HER HEADACHE COULD'VE BEEN THAT BAD. MELANIE WOULD HANDLE THIS, BUT SHE KNOWS THE FAMILY." I WALK INTO THE ROOM. RITA IS MY AGE, BUT SMALL AND THIN UNDER A TANGLE OF DARK HAIR. SHE IS TALKING ON THE TELEPHONE, USED TISSUES LIKE BLOSSOMS LITTERING THE BED, HER HANDS TWISTING THE TELEPHONE CORD LIKE A ROSARY.

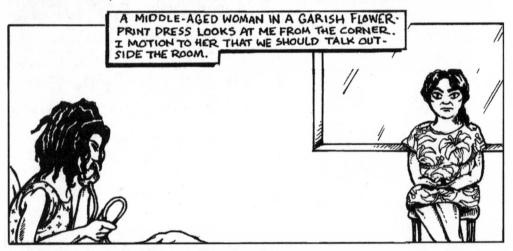

A MIDDLE-AGED WOMAN IN A GARISH FLOWER-PRINT DRESS LOOKS AT ME FROM THE CORNER. I MOTION TO HER THAT WE SHOULD TALK OUTSIDE THE ROOM.

"I AM HER SISTER," SHE SAYS IN A HEAVY ACCENT. I EXTEND A CORDIAL INVITATION FOR THE FAMILY TO COME AND APPLY FOR MEDICAID, SINCE...

"OTHERWISE THE FAMILY IS LIABLE FOR THE ENTIRE BILL."

SHE FROWNS AT ME, FURIOUS, WIPING THE PERSPIRATION FROM HER UPPER LIP. SHE SHAKES HER HEAD RAPIDLY, HANDS FANNING UP AND DOWN, A SUDDEN BREEZE IN THE HALLWAY, TALKS SO FAST I CAN'T MAKE OUT WHAT SHE'S SAYING THE FIRST TIME.

IT'S. JUST. LIKE. RITA, CAUSING. TEENAGE. TROUBLE.

301

DUTY. THAT BOY. MARRY. PAPA TOLD HER. SHE WOULDN'T. I TELL HER, I TOLD HER, GET OVER IT. I DID. I GOT OVER IT.

30

--SHE WHIRLS AROUND, THROWS HER HANDS DOWN "I— I AM HAPPY NOW," SHE SAYS. SHE HOLDS HER HEAD STEADY WITH HER HANDS. SHE LOCKS MY EYES IN HERS AND SAYS,

YOU GET OVER IT. I DID. SHE THINKS SHE'S TOO GOOD.

SHE TURNS ON HER HEEL. SHE CLOSES THE DOOR. I'M ALONE IN THE HALL. I HAVE NOT SET UP AN APPOINTMENT. I DECIDE TO RETURN THE NEXT DAY.

I TAKE THE ELEVATOR TO THE SECOND FLOOR, WALK THROUGH THE DOUBLE DOORS AND INTO THE CAFETERIA. IT IS NOT SO HOT YET THIS MORNING THAT THE IDEA OF COFFEE IS INSTANTLY REPELLANT, AND SO I AM SEATED IN THE SMOKING SECTION, DRAGGING A FINGERTIP AROUND THE STYROFOAM CUP RIM.

YOU GOTTAN EXTRA SMOKE?

I LOOK UP TO SEE THE SPEAKER, A MOON-FACED WOMAN WITH LITTLE ENOUGH HAIR TO BE ENTIRELY CONCEALED BY A BLUE BANDANNA. SHE IS SWALLOWING AND NODDING, GESTURING AS THOUGH SHE IS STILL SPEAKING, BUT SHE HAS FINISHED.

I DRAW A CAMEL FROM THE PACK AND SHE SITS DOWN ACROSS FROM ME. SHE TAKES A CIGARETTE FROM ME, CAREFULLY STANDING IT ON END IN FRONT OF HER. RUNNING HER FINGER AROUND THE ASHTRAY, SHE WITHDRAWS A LONGISH WHITE-FILTERED BUTT AND LIGHTS IT. I GRIND THE REST OF MY CIGARETTE OUT.

"MY STOMACH HURTS. I'M THREE MONTHS PREGNANT," SHE ANNOUNCES, PULLING HER SHIRT UP OVER A DISTENDED STOMACH TO HER BLOATED BREASTS, CONTINUING TO NOD AND GESTURE AFTER SHE HAS FINISHED SPEAKING, YELLOW MOON EYES SWIMMING BACK.

SHE IS OBVIOUSLY MORE THAN THREE MONTHS PREGNANT, BUT I THINK IT BETTER NOT TO ARGUE AS SHE MOANS AND RUBS HER STOMACH.

SHE LIGHTS THE CAMEL WITH THE BUTT, MOANING.

"DO YOU WANT A BOY OR A GIRL?" I ASK, HOPING SHE WILL STOP GESTURING, STOP MOANING OR AT LEAST PULL HER SHIRT DOWN.

SHE DOES NONE OF THESE, BUT STARES ME FULL IN THE EYES, GESTURING MORE EMPHATICALLY.

SHE BLINKS TWICE THEN SAYS,

A BOY. I ALREADY GOT TWO GIRLS.

CAN I HAVE A SIP OF YOUR COFFEE?

I LOOK AT THE WATERY COFFEE AND AT HER MOUTH, AND TELL HER SHE CAN HAVE THE REST.

HER HANDS WRIGGLE IN SMALL TURNING CIRCLES THAT I THINK MEAN "THANK YOU" AS SHE NODS AT ME. SHE BLINKS TWICE.

GOT ANY PILLS?

SHE MUST SEE THE SHOCK FLICKER ACROSS MY FACE BECAUSE HER HANDS BEGIN WRIGGLING AGAIN, SHOULDERS SHRUGGING THIS TIME WHEN SHE SWALLOWS AND SAYS-

Y'KNOW LIKE ASPIRIN? MY STOMACH HURTS.

I'M SORRY, I DON'T. ARE YOU SURE YOU SHOULD TAKE ASPIRIN IF YOU'RE PREGNANT? AND THE SMOKING...

SHE WRIGGLES AND SHRUGS HER RESPONSE, ALL THE WHILE RUBBING HER STOMACH. I RISE FROM THE TABLE, LOOKING AT MY WATCH, MUMBLING SOMETHING ABOUT HAVING TO GET TO WORK.

AS I WALK AWAY SHE IS MUTTERING SOMETHING TO HER HANDS ABOUT-

WHAT KINDA GODDAMN HOSPITAL CAN'T GET NO KINDO DRUGS

WHEN I GET BACK TO THE OFFICE, I TELL LOUISE ABOUT THE WOMAN.

23

WE GET ALL KINDS HERE. WE'RE A PUBLIC FACILITY.

SECURITY CAN GET THEM FOR LOITERING BUT THEY JUST COME BACK. THE BEST THING TO DO IS JUST IGNORE THEM. THEY'RE BASICALLY HARMLESS. IF THEY ASK YOU FOR A CIGARETTE SAY THAT YOU DON'T HAVE ONE OR THEY'LL BOTHER YOU ALL THE TIME.

SHE IS IN THE CAFETERIA AGAIN THE NEXT DAY. I GIVE HER TWO CIGARETTES. SHE DOESN'T LOOK AT ME AS SHE MUTTERS

WHAT KINDA GODDAM HOSPITAL CAN'T GET NO KINDO DRUGS

JOHN EDWARDS: R ARM LACERATION 07189

WOAH. GOOD THING YOU DON'T HAVE TO DEAL WITH THIS ONE.

LOUISE HISSES TO ME IN HER HUSH-HUSH COFFEE BREATH.

"HE WAS IN SOME SORT OF FIGHT WITH HIS GIRLFRIEND, AND STUCK HIS ARM THROUGH HER CAR WINDOW. SHE JUST KEPT DRIVING. THE POLICE FOUND THE GUY SCREAMING AT HER LIKE THE CAR WAS STILL THERE, NOT EVEN REALIZING HOW BADLY HE WAS BLEEDING."

DO YOU THINK SHE'LL COME VISIT HIM?

LOUISE LOOKS AT ME LIKE I AM INCREDIBLY STUPID.

SOMETIMES I THINK I MUST BE STUPID. I AM STUPID ENOUGH TO WANT TO LOVE SOMEONE THAT MUCH SOMEDAY.

STEVE WATSON:
90% 3rd DGR BURNS 071289

LOUISE, COME HERE AND LOOK AT THIS. CHECK OUT THIS DIAGNOSIS.

"LOOK AT THIS. ON THE ER DOCUMENT, IT'S TYPED ACCIDENTAL, BUT ON THE INPATIENT RECORD, IT'S TYPED ZERO."

SHE FROWNS. "ADMITTING MUST HAVE MADE A MISTAKE. SEND BOTH FORMS BACK TO THEM. WHAT DO YOU THINK HAPPENED?" SHE GRABS THE EMERGENCY ROOM DESCRIPTION FORMS FROM THE FOLDER.

"XEROX THE DARKEST COPY OF THIS YOU CAN SO THAT MAYBE WE'LL BE ABLE TO READ IT. I SWEAR TO GOD THE DOCTORS WRITE SO BADLY JUST SO WE CAN'T SNOOP."

GIGGLING, SHE TURNS BACK TO THE MEDICAID VERIFICATION MACHINE AND BEGINS PUNCHING NUMBERS.

WHEN I RETURN WITH THE XEROX, WE PORE OVER THE RUSHED SCRIBBLINGS TOGETHER. LOUISE PULLS A MAP FROM HER DESK, MAKES PENCIL MARKS.

HE LIVES HERE, BUT THE FIRE WAS ON THE ONE-HUNDRED BLOCK OF SOLAR STREET.

"THAT'S A BIG WAREHOUSE DISTRICT. IT'S PROBABLY MAFIA RELATED. THEY TAKE CARE OF A LOT OF BUSINESS AROUND THERE."

SHE REFOLDS THE MAP, SATISFIED WITH HER EXPLANATION, AND GOES BACK TO THE MEDICAID NUMBERS.

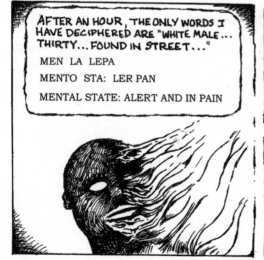

AFTER AN HOUR, THE ONLY WORDS I HAVE DECIPHERED ARE "WHITE MALE... THIRTY... FOUND IN STREET..."

MEN LA LEPA

MENTO STA: LER PAN

MENTAL STATE: ALERT AND IN PAIN

MY STOMACH TURNS, KNOWING WE STILL NEED AT LEAST HIS INSURANCE INFORMATION, AND MORE LIKELY A SIGNATURE. AND IT'S MY JOB TO GO SEE HIM. I'M NAUSEATED THINKING OF HIS BURNED FLESH, CHARRED LIMBS UNDER GAUZE UNDER ICE BUT MY VOICE IS FLIP AS I ASK:

WHAT SHOULD I DO ABOUT THE CHARCOAL ON THE SECOND FLOOR?

LOUISE SCRATCHES HER TEMPLE ABSENTLY WITH THE ERASER END OF THE PENCIL AS SHE SWINGS AROUND IN HER CHAIR.

CHECK FOR A NEXT OF KIN. POKE AROUND UP THERE. I RAN HIS NAME THROUGH THE COMPUTER, AND HE'S MARRIED.

IF HIS WIFE ISN'T AROUND, JUST DROP THE FORMS AT THE DESK. I HOPE SHE'S THERE. THE PAPERWORK'S GOING TO BE HELL IF HE KICKS OFF AND WE DON'T GET A SIGNATURE.

WHEN I LEAVE WORK, I CROSS BEHIND A CAMERA CREW FROM THE LOCAL NEWS, THE REPORTER NOT SWEATING AT ALL EVEN THOUGH HE IS WEARING A SUIT AND IT IS WELL OVER NINETY DEGREES.

I WATCH THE NEWS WHEN I GET HOME

"GOOD EVENING.
TONIGHT, STEVEN WATSON, A NORTH-SIDE RESIDENT, ENTERED HIS WIFE'S PLACE OF WORK AT SYRACUSE LINOLEUM COMPANY. MR. WATSON HANDED A WORKER A NOTE ADDRESSED TO HIS WIFE, THEN PROCEEDED TO EXIT THE BUILDING. A COMPANY EMPLOYEE HAPPENED TO LOOK OUT THE WINDOW AND SEE MR. WATSON IN FLAMES IN THE STREET. HE EXPIRED EARLIER THIS EVENING AT UNIVERSITY HOSPITAL.
HIS WIFE COULD NOT BE REACHED FOR COMMENT, AND THE POLICE WILL NOT DISCLOSE THE CONTENTS OF THE NOTE AT THIS TIME."

THE REPORTER LOOKS SOBER, CONCERNED. THE SCREEN IS FILLED WITH THE IMAGE OF SINGED WHITE SNEAKERS LYING IN THE STREET UNTIL THE COMMERCIAL. I DIDN'T SEE MYSELF PASS IN THE BACKGROUND.

THERE IS NO ONE I LOVE THAT MUCH. NOT YET. MAYBE SOMEDAY.

Q: What do you tell a woman with two black eyes?

A: Nothing. You already told her twice.

I want to tell the perfect American story, about a boy who walked to school with newspaper in his shoes in the Bronx; about a girl who came over during the Holocaust. About a boy who became a man who became a doctor; about a girl who became a model who became a wife. About how they met and fell in love in New York City. I want to tell the perfect American story with three kids and three dogs and a picket fence. But that's not this story.

I don't remember the first time he lost control. I don't remember how many times he lost control. I don't remember much that happened during or right after. And I am still sure it was my fault.

It took me years to think of what happened as abuse - after all, things like that didn't happen in houses like ours. And maybe a spanking or something would have been understandable, a way of disciplining an unruly child. But he beat me with a shoe. Dragged me across the room by my hair. Came at my locked bedroom door with an axe. He did things so bizarre, there was no point in telling anyone - who would believe it? From a man who healed people for a living?

I didn't tell anyone about any of this for years.

I just kept my mouth shut. I walked on eggshells.

Mostly, I kept wishing him dead.

A few years later, it worked.

And I was sure that, too, was all my fault.

Best Friends: True Stories I Would Not Believe

I HAVE A BEST FRIEND. HER NAME IS MAISIE. AND SHE IS BEAUTIFUL AND VERY SMART. WE USED TO GO TO COLLEGE TOGETHER.

me

maisie

I MEET HER IN THE BATHROOM OF MY DORMITORY FRESHMAN YEAR, AS I AM DRUNKENLY VOMITING INTO THE SINK, MUTTERING:

DON'T TELL MY ROOMMATE

WOULDN'T DREAM OF IT, PUMPKIN.

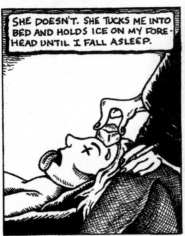

SHE DOESN'T. SHE TUCKS ME INTO BED AND HOLDS ICE ON MY FOREHEAD UNTIL I FALL ASLEEP.

HER FATHER IS A DOCTOR, TOO, I FIND OUT. WE BECOME GOOD FRIENDS.

THEN SHE DROPS OUT OF COLLEGE AND MOVES TO FLORIDA.

LONG DISTANCE, WE DISCUSS WHAT IT IS LIKE TO HAVE DIFFICULT FATHERS WITH LYMPHOMA. SHE HAS MORE EXPERIENCE IN THESE MATTERS, AND SHE TELLS ME

(NUMBER ONE) HOWEVER ANGRY YOU ARE WITH YOUR FATHER NOW, LET IT GO: YOU'LL BE A LOT ANGRIER WHEN HE DIES, AND

(NUMBER TWO) REMEMBER THAT YOU DON'T WANT YOUR FATHER TO DIE: YOU WANT THIS PERIOD OF TIME TO BE OVER.

I TUCK THESE THINGS INTO THE BACK OF MY HEAD, KNOWING AND REGRETTING THAT THEY WILL BE USEFUL.

IT IS JANUARY WHEN I MAKE PLANS TO GO AND VISIT HER IN HER NEW WORLD AND SHE CALLS ME UP A WEEK BEFORE I AM TO LEAVE. I AM WATCHING A MOVIE WITH MY FAMILY. SHE IS CALM WHEN SHE TELLS ME HER FATHER HAS DIED, AND IT WOULD BE AN INOPPORTUNE TIME TO VISIT. THE TEARS CHOKE MY THROAT AND I CANNOT TALK AND EVEN IF I COULD I STILL WOULD NOT KNOW THE RIGHT WORDS TO SAY. I SAY I AM SORRY. I AM THINKING WHAT I WILL TELL MY FATHER WHEN HE ASKS WHY I WILL NOT BE VISITING MAISIE.

29

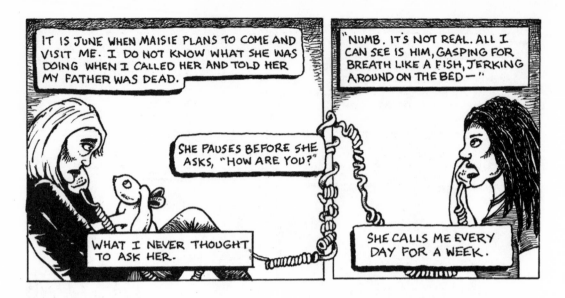

IT IS JUNE WHEN MAISIE PLANS TO COME AND VISIT ME. I DO NOT KNOW WHAT SHE WAS DOING WHEN I CALLED HER AND TOLD HER MY FATHER WAS DEAD.

"NUMB. IT'S NOT REAL. ALL I CAN SEE IS HIM, GASPING FOR BREATH LIKE A FISH, JERKING AROUND ON THE BED —"

SHE PAUSES BEFORE SHE ASKS, "HOW ARE YOU?"

WHAT I NEVER THOUGHT TO ASK HER.

SHE CALLS ME EVERY DAY FOR A WEEK.

MY FATHER HAD A BEST FRIEND. THEY MET AS INTERNS AT MOUNT SINAI, WORKED TOGETHER IN PHILADELPHIA, AND BOTH GRADUATED TO BETTER JOBS IN SYRACUSE. JOE IS CHIEF OF PEDIATRIC HEMATOLOGY, MY FATHER, CHIEF OF HEMATOLOGY AND ONCOLOGY.

OUR FAMILIES GO ON BUSINESS-RELATED TRIPS TOGETHER TO COLORADO, TO NORTH CAROLINA, TO FLORIDA. WE SPEND NEW YEAR'S EVES AT THEIR HOUSE. THEY WATCH NEW YORK GIANTS GAMES ON SUNDAYS AT OUR HOUSE.

NOPE. NOT A DAMN THING.

MY FATHER HAS A HEART ATTACK. JOE CHASTISES HIM FOR WORKING TOO HARD. A FEW WEEKS LATER, JOE'S HEART DOES THE SAME THING. MY MOTHER SUGGESTS THAT FRIENDSHIP IS FRIENDSHIP, KINSHIP IS GREAT, BUT THERE IS NO NEED TO TAKE THESE THINGS TO EXTREMES.

JOE CHOKES THROUGH HIS SPEECH AT MY FATHER'S SERVICE. HE TELLS A JOKE THAT HE SAYS MY FATHER LOVED, A REFRAIN IN THEIR FRIENDSHIP.

"ASK ME TWO QUESTIONS. ASK ME FIRST WHO THE WORLD'S GREATEST COMEDIAN IS, AND THEN ASK ME WHAT THE SECRET OF MY SUCCESS IS."

"WHO IS THE WORLD'S GREATEST COMEDIAN?"

"I AM."

"WHAT'S THE SECRET OF YOUR—"

"MY TIMING."

HE SPITS THROUGH SOBS—

ALAN, YOUR TIMING WAS LOUSY.

HE AND HIS WIFE DO NOT SHOW UP AT THE RECEPTION AT OUR HOUSE AFTER THE SERVICE. WE DO NOT KNOW WHY. TWO DAYS LATER, MY MOTHER GETS A PHONE CALL FROM HIS WIFE. JOE HAS BEEN DIAGNOSED WITH PROSTATE CANCER.

MY MOTHER STARTS EXPLAINING WHAT TREATMENT ENTAILS, BUT CANNOT FINISH A SENTENCE. I ALREADY KNOW. MY DAD WAS A DOCTOR. TREATMENT ENTAILS REMOVAL OF THE TESTICLES AND HORMONE THERAPY; THE PATIENT'S VOICE CHANGES, BODY HAIR DISAPPEARS, AND BREASTS GROW. IF THE PATIENT RESPONDS FAVORABLY TO TREATMENT, HE HAS NO SEX LIFE. IF THE PATIENT IS NOT TREATED OR DOES NOT RESPOND FAVORABLY, HE DIES.

DEATH BY INFILT.

NOPE! NOT A GODDAMNED THING!

THINGS THAT HAPPEN to HE(ART)S

THIS IS A STORY ABOUT TWO BODIES JOINED BY BIOLOGY AND COINCIDENCE. ONE BODY IS IN DECLINE. ONE IS IN A POST-ADOLESCENT HEAT.

ONE BODY IS MY FATHER'S. THE OTHER IS MINE.

THE CANCER ISN'T THE FIRST TIME MY FATHER'S BODY ATTACKS ITSELF. WHEN I'M 10, HE GROWS A SPINAL TUMOR. WHEN I'M 14, HIS HEART STOPS ITSELF.

HE HAD BEEN WORKING OUT WITH MY MOM AND THEY WENT TO A FAST FOOD CHAIN.

I JUST NEED SOME AIR

WHATS WRONG?

A CIGAR, ALAN? WE'RE GOING TO THE EMERGENCY ROOM RIGHT NOW!

THAT'S NOT NECESSARY!!

THIS IS NOT UP FOR DEBATE! I'M GOING TO START THE CAR! NOW!

JUST CALM DOWN, WILL YOU?

THERE WAS NO ONE AT HOME THAT DAY WHEN WE GOT HOME FROM SCHOOL

WHAT THE FUCK

THEY PUT A BALLOON IN HIS CHEST AND BLEW HIS HEART BACK UP, BLEW IT OPEN, SAVED HIS LIFE.

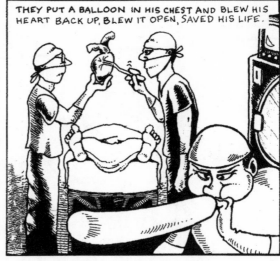

WHAT THIS MEANT TO HIM WAS THAT HE HAD TO GO AND WALK ON A TREADMILL AT LEAST THREE TIMES A WEEK.

WHAT THIS MEANT TO ME WAS THAT I GOT A RIDE INTO THE CITY A FEW TIMES A WEEK

TO GO HANG OUT AROUND THE UNIVERSITY, HIT THE BOOK AND RECORD STORES.

AND THAT'S HOW SOMETHING HAPPENED TO MY HEART FOR THE FIRST TIME.

IN THE RECORD STORE I WALKED INTO, HE TOLD ME HE LIKED THE DAVID BOWIE PIN AND I COULDN'T BREATHE

HE HAD DARK EYES AND ARMY PANTS AND SMOKED VANTAGES!

HE WROTE ME A LETTER. I WROTE HIM BACK. HE WAS IN COLLEGE.

SASHA! ARE YOU SMOKING?

OF COURSE NOT, MOTHER!

BEFORE I KNEW IT, I LOVED HIM

MAYBE EVEN BEFORE I TASTED HIS MOUTH.

IT TASTED LIKE CIGARETTES

I BECAME A DEVOUT SMOKER

SASHA!!

OF COURSE NOT, MOM!

OPEN THIS DOOR!

BLONDIE

HIM

I WAS PROBABLY 15 THE FIRST TIME HE TOOK MY CLOTHES OFF...

SLOWLY, GENTLY,

NOT NEARLY FAST ENOUGH.

I WASN'T SHAKING BECAUSE
I WAS SCARED.

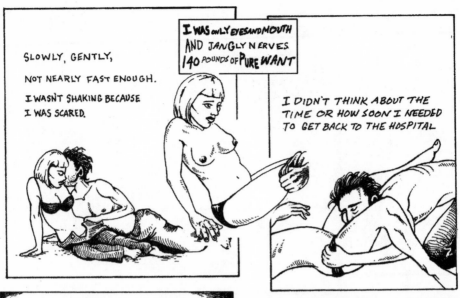

I WAS ONLY EYES AND MOUTH AND JANGLY NERVES 140 POUNDS OF PURE WANT

I DIDN'T THINK ABOUT THE TIME OR HOW SOON I NEEDED TO GET BACK TO THE HOSPITAL

ALL I KNEW WAS HIS MOUTH, HIS HANDS. I TRIED NOT TO STARE AT HIS NAKED BODY. I'D NEVER SEEN A MAN NAKED BEFORE.

WE NEVER FUCKED. WE DID EVERYTHING BUT. WE ROLLED AROUND, OVER AND OVER, ON HIS LIVING ROOM CARPET TO ECHO AND THE BUNNYMEN'S "THE KILLING MOON"

THE KILLING MOON, THE SONG GOES, WILL COME TOO SOON. IT CAME IN THE CARPET. IN HIS HAND. OTHER PLACES. THE KILLING MOON CAME AND CAME. I CAME IN HIS MOUTH.

WHEN HE TOUCHED ME, I GOT THAT CRAZY ROLLERCOASTER FEELING OF EVERYTHING GOING TOO FAST AND WANTING TO PUKE.

THE FIRST TIME I MEET JET SHE COMES GLIDING UP ON HER SKATEBOARD WHILE LOGAN'S HELPING ME MOVE MY STUFF INTO MY NEW APARTMENT. I AM HOME FROM COLLEGE FOR THE SUMMER. BUT I CAN'T LIVE THERE, EVEN THOUGH MY DAD'S DYING.

LOGAN'S CARRYING MY RECORDS UP, AND I'VE GOT MY CAT IN THE CARRIER.

"WHAT'S UP" SHE SAYS. I CAN'T THINK OF ANYTHING TO SAY. I'M TOO BUSY STARING.

LOGAN SAYS "I THINK WE'RE DONE. HOW ABOUT HAPPY HOUR?" HE'S THINKING OF HAPPY HOUR AT JACK'S, WHERE ALL OUR FRIENDS GO. ESPECIALLY NOW THAT IT'S SUMMER AND NO ONE HAS ANYWHERE ELSE TO BE.

"COOL" SHE SAYS. SHE'S BEAUTIFUL. STUNNING. ALL I CAN THINK IS HOW TO GET HER OUT OF HER OVERALLS AND BOOTS. SHE SHAKES HER BEATLES MOP TOP OUT OF HER EYES AND IT FALLS BACK OVER THEM AS SHE KICKS HER BOARD INTO HER HAND.

YEAH, I CAN DO HAPPY HOUR AS LONG AS I CHECK MY MACHINE EVERY HOUR TO MAKE SURE EVERYTHING'S COOL WITH MY DAD.

I LOOK AT JET TO EXPLAIN WHAT'S UP WITH HIM BUT IT'S CLEAR SHE ALREADY KNOWS. LOGAN'S TOLD HER.

WE BRING THE CAT AND THE RECORDS UP AND HEAD TO JACK'S.

IT'S TWO FOR ONE NIGHT AT JACK'S. JACK'S IS MUCH LESS A BAR THAN A BEER-A-TERIA, A ROOM FULL OF PICNIC TABLES AND KEGS. JACK'S IS CRAMMED FULL OF EVERY BROKE COLLEGE STUDENT WHO COULDN'T AFFORD TO GO HOME FOR SUMMER. THEY DON'T CHECK ID'S. WE GET A PITCHER AND GRAB AN EMPTY TABLE.

SO! SO!

SHE WAS GOING TO COMMUNITY COLLEGE AND IS GOING AWAY TO ART SCHOOL IN THE FALL

PEOPLE TRICKLE IN TO THE BAR, YELLING OUR NAMES, GRABBING A SEAT AT OUR TABLE

IT'S 5:30 AND THEY'RE GETTING OFF WORK. SHE'S LIVED HERE ALL HER LIFE.

ALL I CAN THINK IS HOW CAN I WOULD SHE WANT HER HOW maybe...

WE DRINK MORE BEER, AND I GET UP AND CHECK IN AT MY PARENTS' HOUSE AND WHEN I GET BACK, OUR TABLE IS FULL OF FRIENDS AND LOGAN LEANS OVER AND WHISPERS TO ME "BABE! WE NEED TO CHANGE TABLES." I'M CONFUSED.

LOGAN, ALL OF OUR FRIENDS ARE HERE...

LOGAN LIKES BOYS ALMOST AS MUCH AS HE LIKES GIRLS. HE LIKES GIRLS A LOT. I LIKE GIRLS MORE THAN I LIKE BOYS. BUT BOYS ARE EASIER. IT'S SOMETHING WE UNDERSTAND ABOUT EACH OTHER. WHEN WE WERE GOING OUT, WE'D GO OUT LOOKING FOR TOYS TOGETHER. TONIGHT, THOUGH, WE'RE JUST LOOKING FOR A DIFFERENT TABLE. I LAUGH. HE TELLS JET WE'RE MOVING. SHE LOOKS CONFUSED, BUT COMES WITH US.

YEAH HE SAYS, BRUSHING BLUE BRAIDS OUT OF HIS EYES

I'VE FUCKED EVERYONE AT THIS TABLE!

WE FIND EMPTY SEATS AT A TABLE WITH SOME OTHER FRIENDS, A DIFFERENT CIRCLE. WE PUT THE PITCHER DOWN AND DRINK MORE. JET'S WHISPERING IN MY EAR ABOUT THE ARTISTS SHE LIKES, KANDINSKY AND REDON, WHEN I HAVE TO EXCUSE MYSELF.

ONE SEC

TWO THINGS: I HAVE TO CALL MY FOLKS. AND CHANGING TABLES ISN'T ENOUGH. APPARENTLY, WE NEED TO CHANGE BARS.

HYINT!

WHOMP!

HE LOOKS AROUND THE TABLE AND SAYS, "YOU'VE BEEN BUSY!"

THEN SUCKS DOWN HIS BEER AND SAYS "LET'S GO."

FROM THE PAYPHONE, EVERYTHING'S FINE AT MY PARENTS' HOUSE AND MY MOTHER THINKS THAT MY FATHER WILL BE ASLEEP UNTIL MORNING; THERE'S NO NEED TO DRIVE OUT UNTIL THEN. LOGAN BUYS A 6 OF BEER AND WE GO BACK TO MY HOUSE.

HALFWAY THROUGH OUR FIRST BEER, I HEAR LOGAN YELL **FUCK** FROM THE KITCHEN. HIS GIRLFRIEND'S DRIVING INTO TOWN. JET AND I LAUGH.

AND THEN IT'S JUST ME AND JET, SITTING ON THE FLOOR OF MY ROOM.

I DON'T THINK I CAN RIDE MY BOARD HOME

CAN I STAY HERE?

ARE YOU FUCKING KIDDING ME?

KITCHEN CRAP

AND THEN WE'RE KISSING.

AND THEN SHE'S GIGGLING...

40

SHE'S SLIPPING HER HANDS UNDER MY CLOTHES AND SLIDING THEM AWAY.

MY CAT IS STANDING ON HER SKATEBOARD AND WE CRAWL, ELBOW, KNEE, OVER TO THE BED. HER OVERALLS STAY ON THE FLOOR. SO DOES MY SKIRT, MY SHIRT.

HER ARMS STAY AROUND ME AND SHE'S UNDER ME, HER SOFT MOUTH SUCKING MINE LIKE IT'S BREATH, LIKE IT'S LIFE

I CAN FEEL HER NIPPLES AGAINST MY CHEST, HER LEG PUSHING UP INTO ME

AND THEN SHE YELLS

WAIT!!

AND PUSHES ME OFF HER

SHE RUNS OUT OF THE ROOM AND I DON'T KNOW WHY.

THE BATHROOM DOOR

SLAMS

I GRAB A BEER AND WAIT. I DON'T KNOW WHAT TO DO.

41

I FINISH THE BEER.

I OPEN ANOTHER ONE.

SKAPT

I DRINK SOME OF IT.

I PUT IT DOWN.
I WALK TO THE BATHROOM.

JET?

I'M OK. I'LL BE RIGHT THERE.

I DON'T KNOW WHAT I DID WRONG.

I HAVEN'T DONE THIS WITH MANY GIRLS. ENOUGH, BUT NOT MANY.

I GO BACK TO MY ROOM. I TURN ON THE LIGHT AND START STICKING ALBUMS ON SHELVES.

SHE COMES IN PALE

CAN WE TALK FOR A MINUTE?

OF COURSE...

Fuckin' A RIGHT you're gonna talk...

I'VE... I'VE NEVER DONE THIS BEFORE

I DON'T CARE!

NO, THAT'S NOT IT.

WHEN I'M REALLY EXCITED I...

"AND AS LONG AS YOU WANT TO TOUCH ME, I WANT TO BE TOUCHED BY YOU AND— GOD, IT'S OKAY, OKAY?
SHE LOOKS LIKE SHE'S GOING TO PUKE.
"COME ON, GET IN BED" I TELL HER. IT'S GOING TO BE OKAY. IT'S GOING TO BE FINE."

I HOLD HER IN MY ARMS, HER ASS PRESSED AGAINST MY CROTCH, HER FORCEFULLY PRESSING HER SPINE AGAINST MY FRONT, MY NOSE IN HER HAIR AND I WHISPER "IT'S OKAY, IT'S BETTER THAN OKAY."

IT IS MUCH EASIER TO FACE WATCHING SOMEONE YOU LOVE DYING WHEN YOU'VE GOT SOMEONE YOU—SOMEONE YOU MIGHT—WHAT?

SOMEONE YOU REALLY WANT IN YOUR ARMS. AND SHE'S RIGHT THERE. I CAN FEEL HER HEARTBEAT, STRONG, THROUGH HER BACK. WHILE WE'RE ASLEEP, OUR PULSES MURMUR TO EACH OTHER THROUGH THE NIGHT.

IN MY CHILDHOOD HOUSE, CANCER IS MAKING MY FATHER'S HEART STUTTER, GASP, BEGIN TO FAIL. THERE ARE MANY THINGS THAT CAN HAPPEN TO HEARTS. MOST OF THEM TAKE TIME.

Why I HATE Sports

It is March and my father is still well enough to receive visitors. He is coherent and cranky when his friend Moe comes to visit, though conversation is strained. His cancer has gone out of remission, relocated from his neck to his abdomen, something that should never have happened, something that was unexpected..

What do you say to someone who is dying? My father was no longer working, so Moe could not talk about work. Talk about the future that cannot be shared is needlessly painful. Reminiscing about better days is needlessly painful. For him, the "better days" are over. Talk about sports is okay. Someone wins, someone loses, and the contest is finite.

Moe cleared his throat...

THE GIANTS DON'T LOOK LIKE THEY'LL DO TOO WELL NEXT YEAR, DO THEY?

No one said anything. Nobody looked at anyone else. Someone began babbling about the weather.

Childhood Sunday afternoons I am orphaned.
My parents do not answer telephones, walk the
dogs, help with homework, do laundry, or break
up fights between my sister, my brother,
and I. There are more important things to do.

My mother and father have been dating about a year.
My father's time is limited, as he is a resident and "on call"
for days at a time. Three months in a row, my mother
proposes Sunday afternoon dates. Three months in a row
my father declines. Finally, in hurt and frustration, my
mother asks "Who is she?" My father has no idea what she
means.

"Who is who?"

"Look. I don't care if
you're seeing other women
but for God's sake, at least
be honest about who she
is, Alan!"

"I'M NOT SEEING ANYONE
ELSE, ANNE. JESUS."

"Then who are you spend-
ing your Sunday after-
noons with?"

He laughs and looks sheepish, explaining that he
goes to see the New York Giants, he has season tickets,
but not enough money to afford one for her as well.
She buys a season ticket of her own. After all, she's a
working woman. Every autumn Sunday, they huddle
together on the metal bleachers, cheering on a team
that does not frequently win.

46

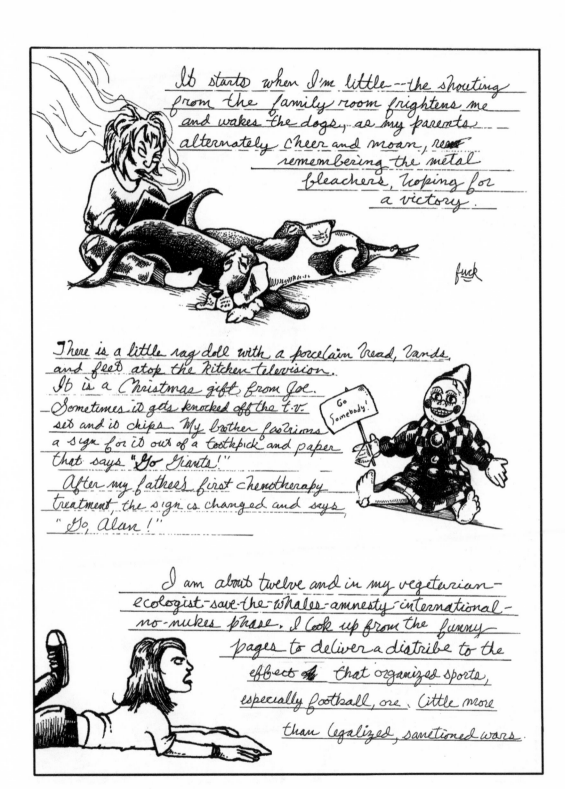

It starts when I'm little -- the shouting from the family room frightens me and wakes the dogs, as my parents alternately cheer and moan, remembering the metal bleachers, hoping for a victory.

fuck

There is a little rag doll with a porcelain head, hands, and feet atop the kitchen television. It is a Christmas gift from Joe. Sometimes it gets knocked off the t.v. set and it chips. My brother fashions a sign for it out of a toothpick and paper that says "Go Giants!"

After my father's first chemotherapy treatment, the sign is changed and says, "Go, Alan!"

Go Somebody!

I am about twelve and in my vegetarian-ecologist-save-the-whales-amnesty-international-no-nukes phase. I look up from the funny pages to deliver a diatribe to the effect that organized sports, especially football, are little more than legalized, sanctioned wars.

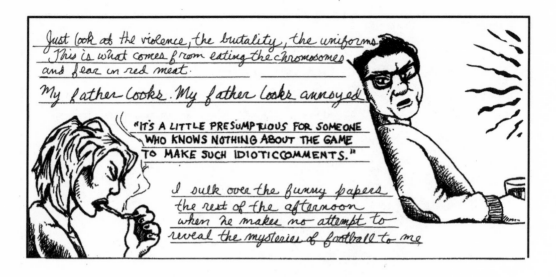

Just look at the violence, the brutality, the uniforms. This is what comes from eating the chromosomes and fear in red meat.

My father looks. My father looks annoyed.

"IT'S A LITTLE PRESUMPTUOUS FOR SOMEONE WHO KNOWS NOTHING ABOUT THE GAME TO MAKE SUCH IDIOTIC COMMENTS."

I sulk over the funny papers the rest of the afternoon when he makes no attempt to reveal the mysteries of football to me.

The television did not go on and I suppose we all knew it was over, although no one could speak those words. My father jokingly called the t.v. his "lifeline." It went on in the morning as soon as he awakened and off at night as soon as he had fallen asleep. It was always tuned to sports. Movies demanded too much attention, sit-coms as well, but he could follow sports. No death scenes, no laugh tracks, and always happy endings, someone always emerging victorious. I hated sports and instead read murder mysteries. We sat in the room from the time he awakened to about midnight, more than one of us not allowed to leave the room at a time, in case he died.

My brother did not go to school. The television did not go on.

It is noon when he rolls his head from side-to-side in drug-heavy confusion, muttering, "Help, help."
My mother grasps his hand, trying to grab something inside him, to tether him to his bed, to the room, to his life.

"I'm here, I'm here, Alan, what is it?"
He opens his eyes wide, panicking.

WHERE'S SASHA?

I move to the bed, crouching next to the bloated shell that hides my father somewhere inside.

THE TEAMS OF TEXAS AND OKLAHOMA ARE TRYING TO RECRUIT YOU. DON'T LET THEM GET HER

His head falls back on the pillow as he screws his eyes shut.

"I'm here, Daddy, I'm here."

HELP. SOMEBODY. HELP.

Later, in the kitchen, my mother explains to me that the teams of both Texas and Oklahoma have been brought up on charges of gang rape, the coaches looking the other way during the proceedings.

An hour later his anti-psychotics have taken effect. The fear is gone from my father's eyes when he opens them. He does not smile when he whispers my name. I move closer to the bed, to near him, to touch him.

"You look beautiful," he says.

"I like the colors in that shirt."

It's a Butthole Surfers t-shirt.

These are the last words my father addresses to me.

It is the day after my father's death, and my family and a few friends are sitting around and drinking. I am doing dishes. I do not feel like sitting or drinking.

My brother and Moe are discussing Michael Jordan and merchandising and fame, my brother saying excitedly, "Wait!" He retrieves a copy of a sports magazine from his room, quickly flipping through until he finds the related article. "Look!"

Moe scans it quickly, nodding, commenting on interesting points, and starts to hand the magazine back to Justin, who buries his hands in his pockets, arms stiff to his sides.

"Here," Moe offers gently.

"No," says Justin, his chin bobbing slightly, "Keep it."

Moe scratches his forehead. "But you might want to read it again."

Justin swallows. "No, please. I need someone to share this with. Please."

Moe looks at the floor and says as jovially as he can,

"Well. Thank you. Thank you very much."

Nobody knows how to restart the conversation. I am finished with the dishes and so I begin to sweep the floor. Until it's dust... to dust... to not sweeping anymore.

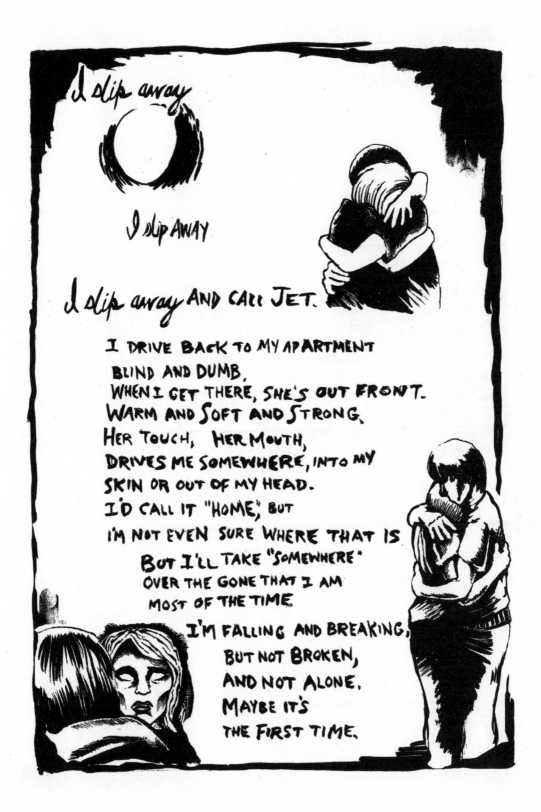

I slip away

I slip AWAY

I slip away AND CALL JET.

I DRIVE BACK TO MY APARTMENT
BLIND AND DUMB,
WHEN I GET THERE, SHE'S OUT FRONT.
WARM AND SOFT AND STRONG,
HER TOUCH, HER MOUTH,
DRIVES ME SOMEWHERE, INTO MY
SKIN OR OUT OF MY HEAD.
I'D CALL IT "HOME," BUT
I'M NOT EVEN SURE WHERE THAT IS

BUT I'LL TAKE "SOMEWHERE"
OVER THE GONE THAT I AM
MOST OF THE TIME.

I'M FALLING AND BREAKING,
BUT NOT BROKEN,
AND NOT ALONE.
MAYBE IT'S
THE FIRST TIME.

how to get the most from your dollar

Syracuse University Hospital		Syracuse University Hotel	
Daily Occupancy		**Daily Occupancy**	
Quadruple:	$260	2 Double Beds:	$103.55
Semi-Private:	$280	1 King	$275
Private:	$340	Suite	$345
Soap, towels, and three meals a day included. Television and telephone at additional charge. Air conditioned/ heated. Floor nursing. Resident rounds.		Toiletries. Turndown service. Complimentary continental breakfast. Complimentary happy hour cocktail. Sauna/jacuzzi/exercise room. Premium cable. In-room fax.	

fashion

Starting about at the age of 14, I would sneak out of the house with my party clothes in my purse or under other clothes. I'd never get out otherwise. My parents kept strange and unpredictable codes about what and how was permissible to wear, codes I could never interpret.

LONG JOHNS UNDER MY SKIRT:
NO ☑

PINK STREAKS IN MY HAIR:
YES ☑

SEE-THROUGH SHIRT WITH BRA:
YES ☑

BRA OVER SHIRT:
NO ☑

 REBELLING IS HARD WHEN THE PARAMETERS AREN'T CLEAR. THE RULES APPLIED MOSTLY TO FASHION, BUT NOT ENTIRELY: CATS WEREN'T ALLOWED, DOGS WERE. FILM CLASSES WEREN'T. CREATIVE WRITING CLASSES WERE.

So, of course, the minute I got to college, I signed up for film classes and got a cat.

AND AT THE END OF THE YEAR, SICK OF TORTURING THE TARANTULA ON MY HEAD WITH HAIRSPRAY AND CRIMPING IRON...
BZZZZZZZZZ

IT FELT GOOD. IT LOOKED GOOD. I KEPT SOME FRINGE IN FRONT, TO STAY EXTRA GIRLIE.
PLEASED with SELF

MY MOTHER DIDN'T SEE IT THAT WAY
!!!!!
WHAT DID YOU DO??
??
IT'S JUST A HAIRCUT

YOU HAD SUCH PRETTY HAIR

DIDN'T THINK ABOUT WHY A SHAVED HEAD WOULD BOTHER HER UNTIL ABOUT A YEAR LATER, WHEN IT ALL GREW OUT, RIGHT BEFORE I TOLD HER I WAS GOING TO GET A
·TATTOO·

OH, ARE YOU GOING TO GET A NUMBER ON YOUR FOREARM?

HOW NICE.

"JUST LIKE ALL THE PEOPLE WHO DIED FOR YOU."

MY MOTHER'S FAMILY CAME TO AMERICA DURING WORLD WAR II.

THEY MADE IT. MANY RELATIVES DIDN'T.

IT WASN'T HER REACTION THAT BOTHERED ME, THOUGH. IT WAS MY FATHER'S. WHEN HE CAME IN, I WAS JUST BACK FROM MY SCHOOL YEAR AND HAD SO MUCH TO TELL HIM.

HE JUST STARED, TURNED WHITE, WOULDN'T SPEAK TO ME. "DAD?" I ASKED. HE TURNED AWAY. "DAD?" HE WOULDN'T ANSWER.

I RAN INTO MY ROOM. I COULDN'T UNDERSTAND WHY HE COULDN'T UNDERSTAND THAT IT WAS JUST A HAIRCUT: MY DAD, OF ALL PEOPLE, WHO WENT TO MEDICAL SCHOOL WEARING BLACK SILK SHIRTS THAT ONLY THE "NEGROES" DARED TO WEAR, NOT POOR JEWISH BOYS FROM THE BRONX; HE, WHO HUNG OUT WITH THE ABSTRACT EXPRESSIONISTS AND SMOKED POT WHEN HE WAS JUST A LITTLE OLDER THAN I WAS; HE, WHO NEVER TALKED OF THOSE DAYS BECAUSE IT MIGHT SOMEHOW CORRUPT HIS KIDS.

HIS KIDS, ONE OF WHOM HAD SHAVED HER HEAD AND NOW LOOKED LIKE THE KIDS IN THE PEDIATRIC CANCER WARD.

EVERY TIME HE LOOKED AT ME, HE SAW A CHILD HE COULDN'T SAVE.

AND REALLY, I WAS THE CHILD HE

COULDN'T SAVE.

I HAD TO BE SAVED FROM HIM

EVERY MORNING, I STILL SAVE MYSELF, REMIND MYSELF THAT THIS IS MY OWN SKIN.

AFTER HE DIED, OVER AND OVER, FOR MONTHS, I HAD THE SAME DREAM: I WAS WALKING DOWN THE SIDEWALK NEAR THE HOSPITAL AND I TURNED A CORNER AND THERE HE WAS—JUST SLIGHTLY IN FRONT OF ME. HE WAS WEARING THE WIG THAT HE WORE AFTER CHEMO STOLE HIS HAIR. HE WAS WEARING A WORK SHIRT AND WORK PANTS AND A PINK KNITTED VEST THAT HIS MOTHER MADE FOR HIM.

IN THE DREAM, I WALKED FASTER AND FASTER TRYING TO CATCH UP. I NEVER GOT ANY CLOSER.

THAT NIGHT, JET MEETS ME AT HOME. WE RACE TO GET OUT OF OUR CLOTHES FAST ENOUGH, GET INTO EACH OTHER FAST ENOUGH *NOTHING IS FAST ENOUGH*

THE CAT RACES ACROSS THE BED, ZIPPING ON AND OFF, NARROWLY MISSING OUR LEGS.

EVERYONE'S EXCITED.

whoop
whoop whoop

MY HAND IS IN HER AND MY MOUTH IS ON HER AND SHE'S CRYING SOFTLY, SWEETLY. SHE'S NOT CRYING LIKE SHE'S HURT. SHE'S CRYING LIKE SHE'S IN A RUINED WORLD BUT SEEING THE BEST IN IT. SHE'S CRYING LIKE SHE'S HERE WITH ME. I LICK HER TEARS AWAY.

SHE'S THE FIRST GIRL I'VE MET WHO SHAVES HER PUSSY. I'M CURLED UP BETWEEN HER LEGS, MY HAND STILL IN HER, MY CHEEK AGAINST THE TOP OF HER TIT. "WHEN DID YOU START SHAVING?" I ASK HER. "WHAT?" SHE ASKS. "SHAVING," I SAY. "WHEN DID YOU START SHAVING YOUR CUNT?" ~~NO ONE~~ NO ONE DID THEN. NOT YOUR MOTHER. NOT PORN STARS.

SHE SIGHED. "WHEN I WAS 10. I DEVELOPED EARLY."

I GOT TEASED A LOT FOR IT. MY UNCLE.

"OKAY," I SAID:

"YOUR UNCLE?"

MY UNCLE STARTED TOUCHING ME

"OH," I said. WHAT ELSE COULD I SAY?

I FIGURED IF HE THOUGHT I DIDN'T HAVE PUBIC HAIR

YET,

HE WOULDN'T FUCK ME

"OH," I said.

WE ARE LYING ON THE BED AND ONLY OUR HANDS ARE TOUCHING. I'M NOT LETTING GO. WE ARE QUIET FOR AWHILE, JUST HOLDING HANDS.

HEY, JET?

I HEAR HER VOICE THROUGH THE DARK, FEEL HER HAND TIGHTEN ON MINE.

what

?

I'VE GOT SOME STORIES for you, too.

Suddenly she rolls on top of me, kissing me, crying, and I hold her and I hold her and I won't stop. We wake up in the morning, she's still on top of me and both our eyes are swollen from crying. It'll take us both years to figure out that we weren't queer because of abuse or molestation. Someday, though, we'll know it. And one of us, maybe both of us, will have it whisper through her skull, in a hot-eyed, angry morning far away,

They didn't win. They didn't win.
I like girls because... I like girls.

and we win. we win.

57

In The Woods Of Forgetting, Alice Can't Remember Her Name.

IN THE PEDIATRIC CANCER WARDS, I DON'T TELL THE KIDS I'M BRINGING THEM COURTESY DISCHARGES. THEY GET CONFUSED AND THINK THEY'RE LEAVING.

"ARE YOU THE TV LADY?"
"NOPE," I SMILED DOWN. "ARE YOU?"
HE LAUGHED. "NO, SILLY. WHO ARE YOU?"

HE LOOKED OUT THE WINDOW, AND WITHOUT WAITING FOR AN ANSWER, POINTED HIS RED LEGO BLOCK AT THE WINDOW, EYES WIDENING, "DID YOU SEE THE HELICOPTER?"

I SURE DID! PRETTY NEAT, ISN'T IT?

WELL, YEAH. BUT IT MEANS SOMEBODY GOT HURT, DOESN'T IT?

I DIDN'T KNOW WHAT TO SAY. I LOOKED FOR HIS MOTHER. "IT MEANS IT'S OKAY NOW; THEY'RE HERE, AND THEY'RE GOING TO GET BETTER. EVERYTHING'S GOING TO BE OKAY."
I THOUGHT OF HIS HEAD BOWED OVER THE SILVER VOMIT PAN, WONDERED WHO HAD MADE HIM THAT PROMISE BEFORE, IF ANYONE COULD HAVE MADE HIM THAT PROMISE. HE WAS UNCONCERNED.

MAYBE THEY GOT EATEN BY A LION AND THAT'S WHY THEY'RE HERE.

MAYBE THE LION ATE SOMEONE AND IT MADE THEM SICK! ALTHOUGH WE DON'T GET MANY LIONS HERE.

MARTY DIDN'T LIKE THAT ANSWER.

THERE ARE LOTS OF LIONS!

HERE? DO YOU THINK SO? I'VE SEEN A COUPLE IN ZOOS, BUT—

HE SHOOK HIS HEAD FROM SIDE TO SIDE SAGELY, THE BARREN HEAD AND PUDGY CHEEKS MAKING HIM LOOK LESS THE SEVEN-YEAR OLD AND MORE THE BUDDHA.

THERE ARE LIONS. YOU DON'T SEE THEM MUCH. BUT THERE ARE LIONS. HERE. I WONDER WHERE THEY PARK THE HELICOPTER.

WHAT'S YOUR NAME?

SASHA

WHAT ARE YOU DOING HERE?

I CAME BY TO SAY "HI," AND TO GET YOUR MOM TO SIGN A COUPLE OF FORMS.

I PUT THE ENVELOPE DOWN ON THE DRESSER

KNOW WHAT MY NAME IS?

OF COURSE. YOU'RE MARTY. MARTY HUNTER.

HE WAS DELIGHTED AND CONTENTIOUS, DROPPING HIS LEGOS IN HIS LAP, FIXING HIS GAZE ON ME.

NOPE. MY NAME IS NOBODY. NOBODY HUNTER.

NO, IT ISN'T

YES IT IS.

NO, IT ISN'T.

HE WAS SINGING TO HIMSELF, GIGGLING.

♪ NOBODY ♪ NOBODY NO-BODY ♪

OKAY, MARTY, WELL, I HAVE TO GO NOW

HE STOPPED SINGING, A BUDDHA'S MEDITATION INTERRUPTED, A GAME LOST.

ARE YOU COMING BACK?

"I'LL STOP BACK TOMORROW. PLEASE GIVE YOUR MOM THE ENVELOPE I LEFT." I START TOWARDS THE DOORWAY. BY THE TIME I REACH IT, HE IS SINGING HIS MULTI-TONED MANTRA,

Nobody No-BODY No...

You are given a name. You are given a life. You grow, you go to school and play with friends, and you grow more and you work and you love and you age.

But what happens when, for some arbitrary reason at some arbitrary age, you are ill, you are more and more dependent, more and more frightened.

You are too sick to work, too sick to play, and the energy you had to love is the energy you have to fear and to hope. To have all the things that were somehow promised is impossible, and you are placed in a room that is not yours, in a dress with no back. Your urine, your blood must be given away. You are poked and prodded by strangers to whom you are not. Your illness is.

What, then, is your name?

"LISTEN, WHEN YOU DROP THAT LETTER TO THE SOCIAL WORKER ON THE SIXTH FLOOR, DON'T SIGN IT WITH YOUR NAME. HAVE YOU NOTICED THE NAME ON MOST OF THE FORMS IS 'M. PIVOT'? THAT'S SO WE CAN KEEP TRACK OF WHICH FORMS ARE OURS, YOU KNOW, WE'RE THE PIVOT DESK, 'M. PIVOT.'"

LOUISE'S PALMS WERE UPTURNED, HER HEAD BENT SLIGHTLY FORWARD, PEERING OVER HER GLASSES TO MAKE SURE I UNDERSTOOD.

THE ONLY ONES THAT ARE DIFFERENT ARE THE ONES THAT ARE FOR CAR ACCIDENTS

SHE WAS WAITING FOR ME TO ASK WHO THEY WERE SIGNED BY. I DIDN'T.

THOSE ARE SIGNED "M. ROADS"

I AM ADVISED TO TURN MY I.D. CARD AROUND, SO THAT MY NAME, MY PICTURE ARE NOT IN EVIDENCE. I DO THIS FOR A FEW DAYS, AFTER THERE HAS BEEN A RAPE ON THE BACK STAIRWELL.

I BEGIN WEARING IT FORWARDS AGAIN WHEN I REALIZE AN ASSAILANT PROBABLY WILL NOT BE INTERESTED IN WHETHER OR NOT I AM PHOTOGENIC, AND PROBABLY NOT CARE WHAT MY NAME IS.

PUDDENTAIN!

FER GIT IT, THEN!

I TURN MY I.D. CARD AROUND WHEN I AM DEALING WITH CANCER PATIENTS, JUST ON THE OFF-CHANCE THAT MY FATHER WAS THEIR DOCTOR. IT AVOIDS QUESTIONS, IT AVOIDS STORIES, AND EVADES MEMORIES.

I TURN MY I.D. CARD AROUND WHEN A MAN I KNEW FROM BARHOPPING IS HOSPITALIZED WITH AIDS.

GOOD MORNING, ROGER. HOW ARE YOU TODAY?

"GOOD. HOW ABOUT YOU?"
"FINE...I NEED YOUR SIGNATURE ON A FEW FORMS..."

HE IS LOOKING AT ME AND HE RECOGNIZES ME BUT IS NOT SURE HOW HE KNOWS ME. WE PLAY STRANGERS.

I AM STANDING IN THE DOORWAY, TRYING TO DECIDE IF THE MAN IN THE PINK SHIRT AND BOW-TIE IS A DOCTOR. HE IS NOT WEARING A LAB COAT, AND HE IS SMILING AND EASY, AFFECTIONATE.

YOU CAN COME IN, YOU KNOW.

I WALK IN AND TELL MR. WALLACE THAT I NEED HIS SIGNATURE. I AM HUNG OVER AND HAVE NOT HAD ENOUGH COFFEE AND I AM NOT TERRIBLY CLEAR IN MY EXPLANATION. HE LOOKS QUIZZICALLY AT THE BOW-TIE MAN.

"WILL I BE SIGNING MY LIFE AWAY?"
"IT'S OKAY, PETE. IT'S JUST FOR BILLING."
HE SMILES AND NODS AT ME, TACIT HELP.

PETE LOOKS AT ME DEFIANTLY.
"AND WHAT IF I DON'T?"
A TROUBLEMAKER.

"THEN THE BILLS GO DIRECTLY TO YOU INSTEAD OF TO YOUR INSURANCE COMPANY. THE WHOLE IDEA IS TO MAKE THINGS AS SIMPLE AS POSSIBLE FOR YOU."

YOU

YOU

YOU

"CAN I JUST PUT AN 'X'?" I AM GLAD THE BOW-TIE MAN WITH THE ROUND GLASSES IS IN THE ROOM. WE NEED TWO WITNESSES FOR ILLITERATES. "MR. WALLACE, YOU CAN SIGN IT, YOU CAN 'X' IT, YOU CAN EVEN DRAW ME A PRETTY PICTURE IF YOU WANT, ANYTHING."
"GO AHEAD, PETE." PETE TAKES THE CLIPBOARD AND BUSIES HIMSELF CAREFULLY READING THE FINE PRINT.

PETE'S QUITE A COMEDIAN. YOU WOULDN'T KNOW BY LOOKING AT HIM THAT HE WILL BE HAVING HIS FIRST HEMODIALYSIS TODAY, WOULD YOU?

I HAD ABSOLUTELY NO IDEA, HE LOOKS SO WELL.

PETE HANDS THE CLIPBOARD BACK TO ME, WITH HIS SIGNATURES UPON THE FORMS.

THIS DOESN'T LOOK MUCH LIKE AN "X" TO ME, MR. WALLACE.

I FELT INSPIRED

I LEAVE, AND MR. BOW-TIE'S VOICE FOLLOWS ME.

ARE YOU THE ONE WHO WRITES POETRY?

I STOP AND TURN AROUND.

THE RESPONSE COMES QUICK, AUTOMATIC. I ANSWER BEFORE I REALIZE I AM SURPRISED BY THE QUESTION.

ARE YOU THE ONE

I USED TO

HE DOES NOT LOOK FAMILIAR, BUT HE HAS SEEN MY NAME TAG AND HE KNOWS WHO I AM AS HE EXTENDS HIS HAND.

"I'M JERRY SHERMAN.
I WANT TO TELL YOU HOW SORRY I AM -- I WORKED WITH YOUR FATHER. WHEN I WAS A RESIDENT, I WAS ON GRAND ROUNDS WITH HIM AND IT WOULD BE SEVEN OR EIGHT AT NIGHT AND WE'D GO INTO A PATIENT'S ROOM AND THE 'NIGHTLY BUSINESS REPORT' WOULD BE ON, AND WE'D WATCH FOR A MINUTE, AND WE WERE BOTH THINKING ABOUT HOW WE WANTED TO GO HOME AND BE WITH OUR FAMILIES.
THEN WE'D BOTH SORT OF SIGH, AND GO ON TO THE NEXT ROOM. HE NEVER LEFT BEFORE EVERYONE HAD BEEN LOOKED IN ON."

"I WANTED TO MAKE IT TO YOUR HOUSE THE WEEK YOU WERE RECEIVING CALLERS, BUT I WAS ON ROUNDS, AND IT WOULD BE SEVEN AND I'D GO INTO SOMEONE'S ROOM AND THE 'NIGHTLY BUSINESS REPORT' WOULD BE ON, AND I REALIZED THAT HE WOULD HAVE BEEN VERY UNHAPPY IF I'D LEFT EARLY."

HE SHRUGS, SUDDENLY A LITTLE BIT SHY, UNCOMFORTABLE. HE LOOKS AT HIS WATCH.

I, UH

"I JUST THOUGHT YOU SHOULD KNOW THAT. PLEASE GIVE YOUR MOTHER AND THE REST OF YOUR FAMILY MY BEST WISHES.
I'VE GOT A MEETING NOW, BUT I'M SURE I'LL SEE YOU AROUND THE BUILDING."

"THANKS," I SAY, AND MIGHT HAVE CONTINUED, BUT HE HAS ALREADY DISAPPEARED DOWN THE CORRIDOR. WALKING DOWN THE HALLWAY, I CHEW THE INFORMATION LIKE SOMETHING SUCCULENT, SOMETHING SUBSTANTIAL.

I SEE THE TWO MEN SILHOUETTED AGAINST NIGHT WINDOWS BY GHOSTLY BLUE GLARE. THEY ARE THINKING OF THEIR WARM KITCHENS.

EXIT STRATEGY

A patient's doctor comes to check in on him on the floor. "Doctor," says the patient, "You've taken out my appendix. You've taken out my spleen. You took out one of my kidneys. You took out part of a lung."

"It's true," said the doctor. "You've had a lot of surgery."

"Doc," says the patient, "All I want to do is get out of here." The doctor nods and smiles. "And you are. Little by little."

Each night, my father sundowns. That's what they call it. He's a little more gone as the sun goes. They call it sundowning the way the sun takes a little bit of every dying patient away with it as it slips below the horizon.

EVEN THE MOON GOES AWAY

This is a strange clock. We can't tell what's coming, only where we've been. How far from here to his death? It's been a year coming so far. How much more time do we have left?

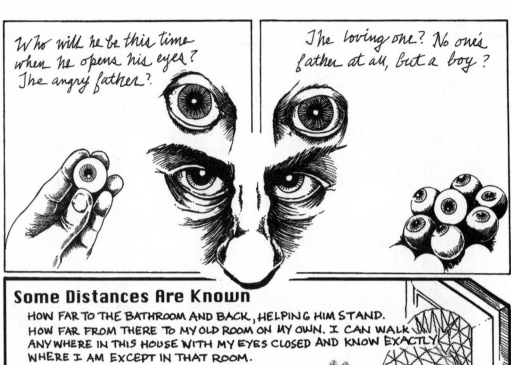

Who will he be this time when he opens his eyes? The angry father?

The loving one? No one's father at all, but a boy?

Some Distances Are Known

HOW FAR TO THE BATHROOM AND BACK, HELPING HIM STAND. HOW FAR FROM THERE TO MY OLD ROOM ON MY OWN. I CAN WALK ANYWHERE IN THIS HOUSE WITH MY EYES CLOSED AND KNOW EXACTLY WHERE I AM EXCEPT IN THAT ROOM.

TOP VIEW

SKY VIEW   θ   CP

NOTHING IN THAT ROOM MAKES SENSE. I CAN'T MEASURE DISTANCE INSIDE IT. ONLY OUTSIDE.

IT IS A HALF HOUR ACROSS THE CITY TO MY APARTMENT. I HAVE BEEN LEAVING EVERY NIGHT AT MIDNIGHT. JET HAS BEEN MEETING ME EVERY NIGHT THERE AT 12:30.

HOW FAR FROM THIS BREATH TO HIS NEXT?

HOW FAR?

TONIGHT WHEN I KISS MY FATHER GOODNIGHT, THEN MY MOTHER, SHE FOLLOWS ME TO MY CAR.

"SASH," SHE SAYS, "HE'S SUNDOWNING PRETTY HARD NOW."

HISTORICALLY, HUMANS MEASURE TIME BY THE SUN.

"HE'S NOT EATING OR DRINKING AND HE'S ON OXYGEN ALMOST ALL THE TIME NOW."

"I KNOW," I SAY.

"MAYBE YOU SHOULD PLAN ON BRINGING SOME MORE STUFF OVER AND SLEEPING HERE FOR THE NEXT FEW NIGHTS," SHE SAYS.

I CAN'T MOVE.
I CAN'T OPEN MY MOUTH.
NOT IN THAT HOUSE.
NOT ONE MORE SECOND.
NOT HIS DEATH.

IF I AM NOT HERE, HE CAN'T DIE.

SHE REACHES OVER AND KISSES ME ON THE CHEEK AND ALL I CAN DO IS NOD, SLAM THE DOOR, DRIVE. I AM BITING DOWN ON MY TEETH SO HARD I AM SURE THEY WILL BREAK. I AM DRIVING 70 MILES AN HOUR DOWN 30 MILE AN HOUR STREETS.

JET'S OUTSIDE MY APARTMENT. SHE PRIES MY LIPS, MY TEETH APART WITH HER TONGUE, IT'S ALL I CAN DO TO NOT TURN MY FACE AWAY, SHOVE HER OFF ME

"STOP," I SAY, SQUEEZING HER HANDS TOO HARD. I UNLOCK THE DOOR AND SHE FOLLOWS ME IN.

I TIGHTEN INTO A BALL ON THE BED AND SHE CURLS AROUND ME. I BREATHE IN AND OUT, SHAKING.
I CAN'T FIGURE OUT HOW TO CRY.

"THERE'S SOMETHING I HAVE TO TELL YOU," SHE SAYS.

I DON'T SAY ANYTHING.

SASH, MY MOM THINKS THAT I'VE BEEN STAYING OUT ALL NIGHT WITH SOME GUY. SHE THINKS I TOLD HER I WAS SLEEPING OVER HERE AS A COVER.

I BREATHE IN AND OUT, SHAKING.

SHE GOT PREGNANT WITH ME AT 16. SHE'S DOING EVERYTHING SHE CAN TO MAKE SURE I GET THROUGH COLLEGE, SHE'S WORKING TWO JOBS...

...I HAVE TO LEAVE FOR BUFFALO IN THE MORNING. SHE'S MAKING ME GO TO MY DAD'S. HE'S GIVING ME A SUMMER JOB FOR SIX WEEKS.

SHE WAITS FOR ME TO SAY SOMETHING I CAN'T.

I'LL BE BACK SO SOON YOU WON'T EVEN MISS ME.

I WHIP OVER. "JET," I SAY. "IT **ONLY** FEELS THAT WAY TO THE ONES WHO GET TO **LEAVE.**"

MAD FEMME
USE EXTREME CAUTION

IT'S OUR LAST NIGHT TOGETHER FOR A MONTH AND A HALF. SHE WANTS LIP AND SWEET AND ALL I AM IS TEETH AND GRISTLE.

WELL, FUCK HER.

ANYTHING YOU SAY CAN AND WILL BE USED AGAINST YOU

"I CAN CALL," SHE SAYS, PANICKED. "I WILL. DO YOU THINK I WANT THIS?" SHE PUTS HER HAND ON MY SHOULDER AND SHOVES ME FLAT ON MY BACK. I ROLL ANGRILY BACK TO MY SIDE. "TELL ME ABOUT DADDY," I SPIT.

"I. WISH. I. COULD.," JET SPITS BACK.

'BUT I CAN'T. HE LEFT WHEN I WAS THREE. *DADDY* IS 2 HALLMARK CARDS A YEAR, ONE AT MY BIRTHDAY, ONE AT CHRISTMAS.
DADDY IS SOMEWHERE MY MOM IS SENDING ME BECAUSE SHE'S SCARED. '

I break like glass breaks; brittle, hard, sharp, not as much crying as shattering into her arms. Fast and done and I kiss her, fierce, hard.

"I'll see you when you get back. I'll probably be here."

I'm telling the truth. I don't know what's coming. Now we're both shaking.

IN THE SMALLEST VOICE I'VE EVER HEARD, SHE PEEPS OUT,

HEY SASH, WHAT'S BIG AND RED AND EATS ROCKS?

I CAN'T TALK. I OPEN AND CLOSE MY MOUTH.

SHE SQUEAKS OUT, "A BIG RED ROCK EATER. WHAT'S BIG AND BLUE AND...EATS...ROCKS?"

A BIG... BLUE... ROCK... eater?

I SOUND LIKE A BALLOON LOSING AIR.

"NO, SILLY," SHE SAYS, MUSSING MY HAIR, HOLDING ME, ROCKING ME, ROCKING HERSELF, HARD, AND TAKING ME ALONG.

"A VERY, VERY SAD BIG RED ROCK EATER"

WE STAY AWAKE ALL NIGHT,

AS MUCH AS WE CAN. WE KNOW THAT SLEEP MAKES MORNING COME BUT WE ARE TOO TIRED AND SLEEP DRAGS US UNDER, COMES ANYWAY, RIPS US APART FROM ONE ANOTHER,

AND SUDDENLY JET IS IN THE LAND OF PLATITUDES AND APOLOGIES, THE LAND OF CHEAP GREETING CARD SENTIMENT AND I AM WATCHING MY FATHER'S LAST BREATHS.

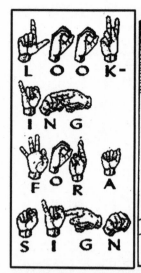

L O O K-
I N G
F O R A
S I G N

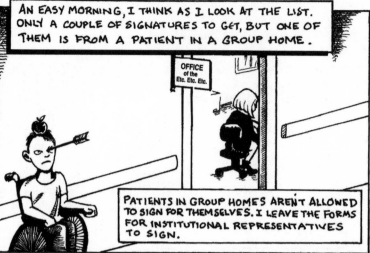

AN EASY MORNING, I THINK AS I LOOK AT THE LIST. ONLY A COUPLE OF SIGNATURES TO GET, BUT ONE OF THEM IS FROM A PATIENT IN A GROUP HOME.

OFFICE of the Etc. Etc. Etc.

PATIENTS IN GROUP HOMES AREN'T ALLOWED TO SIGN FOR THEMSELVES. I LEAVE THE FORMS FOR INSTITUTIONAL REPRESENTATIVES TO SIGN.

THERE WAS A BOY ON MY JUNIOR HIGH SCHOOL BUS WHO LIKELY WENT TO A GROUP HOME AFTER SPECIAL ED. HE COULD HIT ANYBODY HE WANTED WHENEVER HE WANTED, AND HE COULD CRY AFTER A BAD DAY, AND IT WAS ALL RIGHT. EVERYONE UNDERSTOOD. I WAS ALWAYS A LITTLE BIT JEALOUS OF HIM, TO TELL THE TRUTH.

I CHECK THE NAME PLATES ON THE DOOR, JUST TO MAKE CERTAIN THAT I HAVE THE RIGHT ROOM.

SOMETIMES THEY SHUFFLE PATIENTS INTO DIFFERENT ROOMS OR INTENSIVE CARE WARDS WITHOUT ENTERING THESE CHANGES INTO THE COMPUTER; I HAVE THE CORRECT ROOM, AND MR. WILLIAM HIBBARD'S BED IS ON THE FAR SIDE OF THE ROOM.

I SEE THE MACHINE FIRST WHEN I OPEN THE DOOR, HULKING AND IMPOSING, COMPLETE WITH FLASHING LIGHTS AND BEEPING NOISES.

Beep

THERE IS A DOCTOR. HE IS WEARING A WHITE COAT, STANDING AT THE FOOT OF THE BED, A BARE FOOT IN ONE OF HIS HANDS.

HE IS SLAPPING IT, LIGHTLY, THREE TIMES, THEN LOOKING AT THE MACHINE, IN SOME SORT OF RHYTHM I AM NOT AWARE OF.

THE FOOT IS ATTACHED TO A MAN— I CATCH MY BREATH FOR A SECOND, THINKING HE IS DEAD—HE IS NOT MOVING—HE IS SWEATING PROFUSELY, HIS MOUTH AGAPE, HIS EYES FLOATING IN THE HOLLOWS OF HIS HEAD.

BUT THE DOCTOR IS CALM AS HE TURNS TO ME, TAKING IN MY SHOES, MY LEGS, MY DRESS, MY FACE, HE IS DARKLY HANDSOME AND SWARTHY.

CAN I HELP YOU?

THERE IS NO CRISIS. HE IS CALM.

I HAVE FORGOTTEN WHY I AM IN THIS ROOM, WATCHING THE SLAP-SLAP-SLAP OF HIS HANDS ON THE FOOT, THE FLASH AND HUM OF THE MACHINE, THE OPEN MOUTH, THE SWEAT, THE STARING EYES.

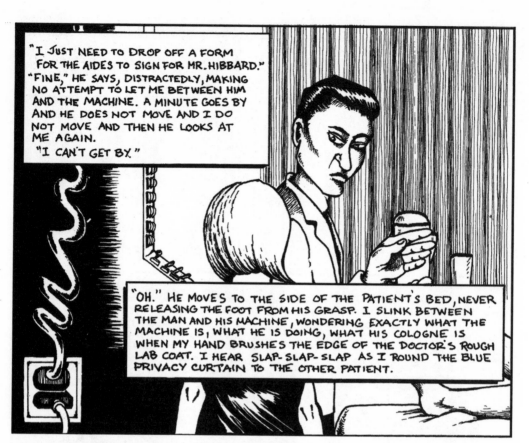

"I JUST NEED TO DROP OFF A FORM FOR THE AIDES TO SIGN FOR MR. HIBBARD."
"FINE," HE SAYS, DISTRACTEDLY, MAKING NO ATTEMPT TO LET ME BETWEEN HIM AND THE MACHINE. A MINUTE GOES BY AND HE DOES NOT MOVE AND I DO NOT MOVE AND THEN HE LOOKS AT ME AGAIN.
"I CAN'T GET BY."

"OH." HE MOVES TO THE SIDE OF THE PATIENT'S BED, NEVER RELEASING THE FOOT FROM HIS GRASP. I SLINK BETWEEN THE MAN AND HIS MACHINE, WONDERING EXACTLY WHAT THE MACHINE IS, WHAT HE IS DOING, WHAT HIS COLOGNE IS WHEN MY HAND BRUSHES THE EDGE OF THE DOCTOR'S ROUGH LAB COAT. I HEAR SLAP-SLAP-SLAP AS I ROUND THE BLUE PRIVACY CURTAIN TO THE OTHER PATIENT.

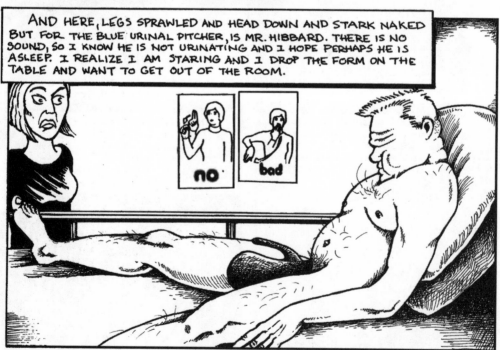

AND HERE, LEGS SPRAWLED AND HEAD DOWN AND STARK NAKED BUT FOR THE BLUE URINAL PITCHER, IS MR. HIBBARD. THERE IS NO SOUND, SO I KNOW HE IS NOT URINATING AND I HOPE PERHAPS HE IS ASLEEP. I REALIZE I AM STARING AND I DROP THE FORM ON THE TABLE AND WANT TO GET OUT OF THE ROOM.

I FORGET ABOUT THE MACHINE AND THE MAN UNTIL I ROUND THE CURTAIN AGAIN AND I HAVE TO STAND THERE UNTIL HE MOVES ASIDE FOR ME.

SHOULDN'T SOMEONE BE IN THE ROOM WITH HIM?

THE DOCTOR SAYS NOTHING, STILL SLAPPING AND MANIPULATING A TOE IN HIS HAND.

"THANKS," I SAY, TRYING NOT TO RUN OUT OF THE ROOM. I HEAR A GRUNT THAT IS SOME SORT OF ACKNOWL-EDGMENT AS I CLOSE THE DOOR BEHIND ME.

I AM DOWN THE HALL, LOCKED IN THE LEMONADE-YELLOW BATHROOM STALL FUMBLING FOR MY CIGARETTES WHEN I REALIZE I LEFT THEM IN MY DESK.

GAH DAMMIT!

I STAND THERE FOR A MINUTE ANYWAY, TRYING TO ERADICATE THE FOOT, THE BLUE URINE PITCHER, THE DOCTOR'S HEAVY COLOGNE AND SLAPPY HANDS FROM THE WALL I AM FACING.

I HEAR THE BATHROOM DOOR SWING OPEN AND KNOW THAT SOME-ONE ELSE HAS COME IN THE BATH-ROOM SO I FLUSH AND WASH MY HANDS, JUST FOR APPEARANCE'S SAKE.

AND THEN I GO TO THE NEXT ROOM.

THE PRIVACY CURTAIN SHIELDS THE BED FROM MY VISION. I LISTEN FOR THE BEEPING OF A MACHINE, FOR A SLAP-SLAP-SLAP BUT DO NOT HEAR IT, AND I AM SOMEWHAT COMFORTED.

IT'S A MAN WITH A HUGE BELLY. HE IS WEARING A LAUGHABLY SMALL PAIR OF BURGUNDY JOCKEY SHORTS. HE IS SNORING, AND IT IS SOMETHING COMFORTABLE, FAMILIAR AS THOUGH HE HAD BEEN WATCHING A BASEBALL GAME ON TELEVISION AT HOME AND HAD FALLEN ASLEEP.

I RETURN TO THE OFFICE SIGNATURELESS. LOUISE HAS NOT LEFT YET. THERE IS NOT MUCH TO DO, BUT MELANIE IS IN A MEETING AND JUDY'S CAR BROKE DOWN, AND BESIDES,

LOUISE SAYS SHE CAN USE THE OVERTIME. SHE TELLS ME I SHOULD GO UP TO ROOM 315 AND SEE THE MAN IN THERE.

WE DON'T REALLY NEED A SIGNATURE SINCE HE'S ON BLUE CROSS, BUT,

"HE'S REALLY STRANGE LOOKING. I'VE NEVER SEEN ANYONE DEFORMED LIKE THAT BEFORE. OF COURSE, I'M NOT OUT ON THE FLOOR AS MUCH AS YOU, SO I DON'T SEE THAT MANY UNUSUAL THINGS, BUT **STILL**, SASHA, HIS BODY'S TOTALLY NORMAL DOWN TO HIS ELBOWS AND THEN HE DOESN'T HAVE ANY FOREARMS, JUST TINY LITTLE BABY HANDS STICKING OUT AT NINETY DEGREE ANGLES — I THINK HE MUST'VE BEEN A THALIDOMIDE BABY. CAN YOU IMAGINE GOING THROUGH LIFE LIKE THAT? I WONDER HOW HE'D SIGN A FORM."

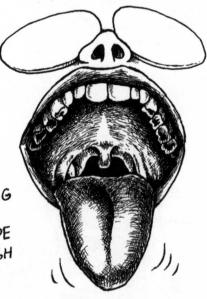

SHE CHEWED ON THE END OF HER PEN, HER EYES DISTANT, TRYING TO PICTURE THE POSITION IN WHICH THE MAN COULD HOLD A PEN.

I AM GLAD THERE ARE ONLY TEN MINUTES LEFT IN THE DAY.

YOU KNOW WHAT? I'M TOO BUSY RIGHT NOW.

THE HEAVY WET HEAT OF THE AIR IN THE HALLWAYS ALMOST MAKES ME SICK IN THE MORNINGS. IT IS COTTON, IT IS DISINFECTANT, IT IS VERY HOT IN THE CORRIDOR, AND FAR TOO HOT FOR COFFEE TODAY, WARM AIR RIPPLING PINK RIBBONS TIED TO THE NURSES' STATION DESK FAN.

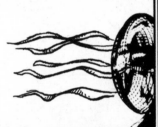

THERE IS A MAN SITTING IN A VINYL EASY CHAIR FACING THE NURSES' STATION DESK FAN. AS I WALK CLOSER, I SEE THAT HE IS TIED TO THE CHAIR BY A WHITE SHEET WHICH IS KNOTTED IN THE BACK IN A BIG BOW. HE IS JERKING FORWARD AND BACK, SLOWLY.

I AM WALKING BY WHEN HE GRABS MY SLEEVE.

HARD.

THE BOUND MAN HAS MY SLEEVE AND I YANK IT LOOSE AND HE SAYS,

"HAEY?"

HAEY?

WHEN I TURN AND LOOK, HE IS PLACID AND SWEET, THE WORLD'S OLDEST BABY.

No ONE EVER MENTIONED TO ME THAT THEY TIED PATIENTS, EVEN THE PATIENTS FROM GROUP HOMES, TO FURNITURE.

"WE JUST DON'T HAVE THE STAFF THAT WOULD ALLOW US ONE-ON-ONE CARE, AND THESE PEOPLE NEED TWENTY-FOUR HOUR SUPERVISION. THEIR OWN FACILITIES CAN'T SPARE THE PERSONNEL TO CARE FOR THEM HERE. WHAT ELSE COULD WE DO? THEY DON'T MIND, THEY GET LOTS OF ATTENTION THIS WAY, FROM EVERYONE WHO WALKS BY. I DON'T SEE WHY YOU'RE SO UPSET ABOUT THIS, IT'S NOT LIKE WE'RE MISTREATING THEM."

"Hi...?" HE SAYS. "HAEY?"

HE IS TALKING TO ME AND I CAN'T UNDERSTAND HIM.

Heebo. Heevo. Heyvar.

I SAY "HEYVAR" AND NOD AND SMILE. I HAVE ABSOLUTELY NO IDEA WHAT HE MEANS.

HEYVAR!

HE IS POINTING AT HIS WRIST AND I NOD AND SMILE AND THEN I SEE WHAT HE IS TRYING TO SHOW ME, HIS HOSPITAL BAND, **HIBBARD, W.**

"HIBBARD! YOU'RE MR. HIBBARD!"

AND HE IS DELIGHTED AND SMILING. "HEEBO, HEEVA!"
I NOTICE HE IS ALLOWED TO WEAR HIS OWN LIGHT BLUE PAJAMAS.

"S-SIGN? YOU? S-SEE? S-SIGN?"

HE HAD NOT BEEN SLEEPING WHEN I DROPPED THE ENVELOPE OFF YESTERDAY.

"YOU, DRESS, BLUE, GOOD." HE IS POUNDING HIS THUMB ON HIS CHEST, A LITTLE TOO HARD, JERKING FORWARD AND BACK.

"MAY? S-SIGN? HEYVAR!"

HE WANTS TO SIGN THE FORM.
I TAKE A DEEP BREATH.

HEYVAR!

"OH, DON'T YOU WORRY ABOUT THAT! IT'S ALL BEEN TAKEN CARE OF, MR. HIBBARD!"

"WE DON'T NEED YOU TO SIGN IT ANYMORE. NOW, YOU FEEL BETTER SOON. BYE!"

MY TONE IS SO SACCHARINE SWEET I'M CHOKING ON IT.

I BITE THE INSIDE OF MY CHEEK, STARE AT THE DOOR TO THE STAIRS, "HEYVAR! ME! HEYVAR!" FOLLOWING ME,

AND IT ISN'T UNTIL I GET DOWNSTAIRS THAT I REALIZE I SHOULD'VE LET HIM SIGN THE DAMN THING. NO ONE WOULD HAVE EVER KNOWN THE DIFFERENCE, NO ONE EXCEPT HIM AND ME WOULD HAVE CARED.

HEYVAR

So this bear walks into a bar. The bear says, "I'd like a beer."
The bartender says, "I'm sorry, sir. We don't serve beers to bears in
Boise, Idaho."

The bear looks to his left. There's a small, meek man sitting at a nearby
table. The bear looks at the man, licks his lips and goes CHOMP! and eats him
up in a single bite.

The bear wipes his mouth with the back of his paw and looks at the
bartender. "Sir," he says, "I don't think you heard me. I said I'd like a beer."

"Sorry," says the bartender, shrugging. "We don't serve beers to
bears in Boise, Idaho."

The bear looks to his right, where there's a portly traveling salesman
sipping his whiskey. The bear looks at the man, licks his lips and goes
CHOMP! and eats him up in a single bite.

The bear wipes his mouth with the back of his paw and looks at the
bartender. He shakes his head slowly from side to side. "Dude," says the bear,
"I'm starting to get a little pissed off here. And you wouldn't like me when I'm
pissed off. Now Gimme A Beer."

"Sorry," says the bartender, shrugging. "We don't serve beers to bears in
Boise, Idaho."

The bear looks to his left again, where a young, comely woman is leaning
against the bar, smoking a cigarette. The bear looks at the man, licks his lips
and goes CHOMP! and eats her up in a single bite.

"I'VE HAD IT, PAL," yells the bear. "GIMME THAT BEER!" "Sorry, sir,"
says the bartender.
"We don't serve beers
to drug addicts in
Boise, Idaho."

"Drug addicts?!?!?"
yells the bear.
"What do you mean
drug addicts?!?!"

"That's the
bar bitch
you ate."

another joke

MOVING VIOLA-TIONS

LOGAN, I'M TAKING OFF.

"CAN'T YOU WAIT TWENTY MINUTES? HANG ON--" HE SLIPS THE HEADPHONES OVER HIS EARS AND SPINS THE RECORD INTO PLACE, THEN FLIPS THE TOGGLE SWITCH. THE SONG IS TOO LOUD, INTONING, "GIRL, I'LL HOUSE YOU - GIRL, I'LL HOUSE YOU--GIRL--," IN THE CROWDED BAR. PEOPLE WRIGGLE IN TIME, ARCH AND POUT, AND NO ONE SMILES. IT IS TOO HOT, AND THE PACKED, SMOKY ROOM IS PRESSING UP TOO CLOSE AGAINST ME.

"I'LL BE OUT OF HERE IN TWENTY. YOU ALWAYS GIVE ME A RIDE HOME". LOGAN PUSHES HIS HAIR FROM HIS DARK EYES .

"HANG OUT. GO GET A DRINK. ON ME. I'LL START PACKING SHIT UP.

PLEASE?"

PLEASE?

THE MUSIC IS TOO LOUD, THE DRONE OF THE BASS AN ANNOY-ING BUZZ UP MY SPINE.

"GIRL I'LL HOUSE YOU -
GIRL I'LL FUCK YOU -
GIRL -"

LOGAN HAS IMPRESSIVELY DARK EYES AND SOMETIMES I THINK HE IS MY BEST FRIEND AND SO I SAY OK, EVEN THOUGH I AM ANGRY AT HIM FOR TELLING A BOUNCER I AM A DYKE. HE RATIONALIZES IT TO ME, CALMLY EXPLAINING,

"HE'S A JERK, SASHA, BELIEVE ME. WHAT, DID YOU WANT HIM TO ASK YOU OUT?"

WHAT?

I AM TIRED. I HAVE TO BE AT WORK IN SIX HOURS. MY BODY IS HEAVY, FULL OF HURT THE WAY I DIDN'T KNOW IT WOULD BE ON THE TWELFTH OF EVERY MONTH. "OKAY, LOGAN. I'LL GO GET THE CAR AND PULL IT AROUND SO YOU CAN LOAD YOUR RECORDS IN." I DON'T WANT TO BUT WHATEVER. MY HEAD IS HEAVY AND I SLAM TIGHT THE CAR DOOR, LOCK MYSELF INSIDE, ALONE.

IT ISN'T UNTIL I TURN THE CAR OFF THAT I SEE THE FLASHING RED LIGHTS IN MY REAR VIEW MIRROR, CYCLING LIKE A PULSE.

"IS THERE A PROBLEM, OFFICER?"
I SMILE WEAKLY.
"LICENSE AND REGISTRATION."
HE IS NOT SMILING.
"IS THERE A PROBLEM, OFFICER?"
I SMILE WEAKLY.
"LICENSE AND REGISTRATION."
HE IS NOT SMILING.
"COULD YOU PLEASE TELL ME WHAT THE PROBLEM IS?"

"LICENSE AND REGISTRATION." HE IS ANNOYED. I HAND HIM MY LICENSE AND REGISTRATION AND HE GOES BACK TO HIS CAR. I SIT IN MY CAR FOR THE MINUTES THAT FEEL LIKE HOURS UNTIL HE COMES BACK.

COULD YOU PLEASE TELL ME WHAT I DID WRONG?

MY STOMACH IS SOUR-SICK FROM THE TOM COLLINS.

I AM GLAD HE DOES NOT SMELL THE ALCOHOL ON MY BREATH AS HE LEERS NASTY INTO MY CAR.

"OH, SO YOU HAVE NO IDEA THAT YOU JUST BLEW THROUGH TWO STOP SIGNS?" HIS EYES ARE SQUINTY AND SARCASTIC. I DO NOT WANT TO CRY AS HE GOES BACK TO HIS CAR TO GET HIS TICKET BOOK, BUT I CAN FEEL MY THROAT TIGHTEN AS I GET OUT OF MY CAR, FOLLOWING HIM.

 LOOK, I'M REALLY NOT A CARELESS DRIVER -- I'VE NEVER GOTTEN A TICKET BEFORE AND I JUST CAN'T GET ONE AND I'M REALLY TIRED AND REALLY UPSET AND I REALLY DIDN'T SEE THE SIGNS AND —

 WHERE ARE YOU COMING FROM TONIGHT?

 I WAS HANGING OUT WITH FRIENDS IN THERE. I WAS JUST GETTING—

 HOW MUCH HAVE YOU HAD TO DRINK?

JUNIOR SPACEMAN

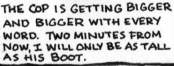 THE COP IS GETTING BIGGER AND BIGGER WITH EVERY WORD. TWO MINUTES FROM NOW, I WILL ONLY BE AS TALL AS HIS BOOT.

 I ONLY HAD ONE

DRINK

IT IS A

LIE

 HOW DO YOU FEEL ABOUT HAVING A BREATHALYZER?

 I ONLY HALF-NOTICE WHEN LOGAN COMES OUT OF THE BAR, PUTS A BOX OF RECORDS INTO THE CAR, AND GOES BACK INSIDE. I DO NOT WANT TO SHRIEK AT HIM.

 LOOK. PLEASE -- MY FATHER DIED EXACTLY ONE MONTH AGO TONIGHT AND I JUST WANT TO GO HOME AND CAN'T YOU JUST—

THE RADIO AT HIS HIP GOES OFF. HIS FACE DOESN'T CHANGE. HE DOESN'T MOVE. HE LOOKS AT ME.

THAT YOUR FRIEND?

HE PUSHES HIS CHINS IN LOGAN'S DIRECTION

"YEAH," I SAY. I AM SHOCKED THE COP CAN HEAR ME ALL THE WAY UP THERE, HIS EARS FIFTY FEET HIGH IN THE AIR.

"DOES HE DRIVE?" "YEAH," I SAY.

I'M GONNA LET YOU OFF WITH A WARNING THIS TIME, BUT HE'S DRIVING HOME TONIGHT. AND BE CAREFUL!

I HAVE STOPPED CRYING BY THE TIME LOGAN COMES BACK, PIZZA BOX IN HAND

YOU LOOKED HUNGRY. LET'S GO TO MY HOUSE, SASH.

OKAY. BUT YOU'RE DRIVING. THE COP SAYS SO.

WOPPO'S PIZZA

HE STOPS AT EVERY STOP SIGN FOR AT LEAST THIRTY SECONDS. MY BONES DISSOLVE AS I SIT IN THE PASSENGER SEAT. I AM A BAG OF BLOOD.

ONE - ONE THOUSAND TWO - ONE THOUSAND...

WE FINISH THE WHOLE PIZZA, GREASY WITH MUSHROOMS AND SAUSAGE. LOGAN STROKES MY HAIR AND DOES NOT MAKE ME TALK.

"LET'S GO UPSTAIRS"

SOMETIMES I THINK LOGAN IS MY BEST FRIEND.

HE DOES NOT MAKE ME TALK. HE HANDS ME HIS SNOOPY AND UNDRESSES, HIS BACK PALE AND THIN, HIS PALE BLUE BOXER SHORTS BALLOONING AROUND HIS HIPS.

I AM TIRED, SHEETS COOL AROUND MY LEGS, PILLOW UNCOMFORTABLY HIGH UNDER MY HEAD. THERE'S ALWAYS SOMETHING DISCONCERTING ABOUT FOREIGN BEDS. THEY DO NOT SMELL QUITE RIGHT, AND THE SHEETS ARE A LITTLE TOO ROUGH OR LIMP AGAINST THE SKIN. I AM TOO TIRED TO LET THIS MATTER.

"WHAT TIME DO YOU NEED TO GET UP?" HE ASKS, SETTING THE ALARM CLOCK. HE KNOWS THE ANSWER BUT ASKS ANYWAY, HOPING IT WILL NOT BE SEVEN O'CLOCK.

THE CLICK OF A SWITCH AND DARK. LOGAN'S BREATH DAMP ON THE NAPE OF MY NECK, KNEES TUCKED INTO BACK LEG HOLLOWS.
HIS FINGERTIPS TRAVEL ACROSS MY STOMACH LIKE A SCHOOL OF FISH, DARTING OVER AND BACK, ONE SLIDING UNDER THE ELASTIC WAISTBAND ON MY HIP.

MY LEG SWINGS BACK FROM THE KNEE, KICKS HIM IN THE ANKLE.

CUT IT OUT, LOGAN. I HAD A TERRIBLE NIGHT.

"YEAH. I WAS THERE, REMEMBER?" HE TUGS THE ELASTIC AWAY FROM MY HIP, PRESSES TIGHTER AGAINST ME

CAN'T WE JUST GO TO SLEEP?

LOGAN IS BITING THE BACK OF MY NECK AND HE IS NOT GOING TO ANSWER ME. I DO NOT FEEL LIKE HAVING SEX, I FEEL LIKE BEING MISERABLE OR NOT EVEN THAT BUT SLEEP-NUMB AND HEAVY-HEADED, I WANT TO SLIP INTO A QUIET LIKE WATER.

HIS HAND BUNCHES MY SHIRT UP IN BACK, TUGS IT TO MY SHOULDERS.

JESUS, LOGAN. WHAT ABOUT JET?

JET WON'T CARE. YOU KNOW THAT.

c'mon i'm your best friend

"YEAH," I SAY. "I GUESS."
SHE WON'T. WE TALKED ABOUT IT.
WHETHER OR NOT WE CARE, RIGHT
NOW, NEITHER OF US GETS THAT
CHOICE; SHE'S AWAY FOR A MONTH,
AND THEN WE HAVE A COUPLE OF
WEEKS BEFORE WE BOTH GO BACK
TO SCHOOL HOURS AWAY FROM
EACH OTHER. IT MAKES SENSE
FOR US TO SEE OTHER PEOPLE.
BUT THAT'S NOT THE POINT.

"YEAH," HE SAYS. "SO..." HE SAYS.

I WISH HE WAS JET. I WISH JET WAS HERE. I WISH I WAS HOME,
ALONE. HE'S STILL TUGGING AT MY UNDERWEAR. AND I AM SO TIRED.
I GIVE UP. NOTHING MATTERS.

The pizza is a rock in my belly
and Jet's gone and my bones
are gone and my dad is dead.

And so we have sex...

... and I respond as much as I have to, make a little
bit of noise and rock my hips against him, tighten
myself around him and then it is over fast and
I can go to sleep.

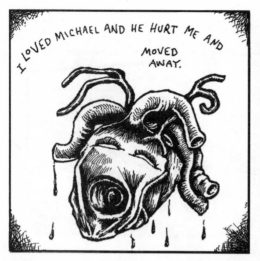

I LOVED MICHAEL AND HE HURT ME AND MOVED AWAY.

I loved Theo and we hurt each other and then he moved away.

STEVE AND I NEVER KNEW WE LOVED EACH OTHER UNTIL HE MOVED AWAY AND WE ONLY KNEW IT BECAUSE WE HURT.

I LOVED CHRISTINE, MY BEST FRIEND, AND THEN WE WENT AWAY TO COLLEGE AND SHE CHANGED AND I CHANGED AND NOW EVERY TIME WE SEE EACH OTHER,

It Hurts.

I loved Floyd, our puppy, and then he drowned, and it hurt.

TNT

I loved my father and he died and it still Hurts.

AND SO I DECIDED THAT I WAS NOT GOING TO HURT ANYMORE.

DAN IS FLIRTING WITH ME AS HE HAS FOR THE PAST THREE YEARS, AND I WANT HIM TO STOP. I SEE HIM AT A PARTY AND WE GO BACK TO MY APARTMENT. WE HAVE ANGRY SEX WITH OUR CLOTHES ON AND THEN I DRIVE HIM HOME TO HIS WIFE. HE DOES NOT FLIRT WITH MY ANYMORE. WE DO NOT SPEAK ANYMORE. AND THIS DOES NOT HURT.

HEATHER RUBS UP AGAINST ME IN BARS, TOUCHES ME TOO MUCH, MAKES FUN OF HER BOYFRIEND TO PROVE HOW MUCH SHE'S INTO GIRLS AND ALWAYS GOES HOME WITH HIM AFTER WHISPER-ING "CALL ME" IN MY EAR AND STICKING HER TONGUE IN MY MOUTH. THIS DOES NOT HURT.

WHEN ERIC AND I MEET IN A BAR, I BRING HIM HOME WITH ME BUT WILL NOT LET HIM TOUCH ME. WE DISCUSS POLITICS, FEMINISM, THE MILITARY, WAR, AND DEATH. I LET HIM DRIVE ME TO WORK THE NEXT MORNING, AND TAKE ME OUT TO DINNER THE NIGHT AFTER. I STILL DO NOT LET HIM TOUCH ME. WHEN THE WEEK AFTER, HE SENDS ME A LOVE LETTER, I STOP TALKING TO HIM, AND WILL NOT ANSWER HIS PHONE CALLS. HE DOESN'T STOP BY ANY MORE. AND THIS DOES NOT HURT.

MEG STOPS BY ONCE IN A WHILE LATE AT NIGHT WHEN SHE HAS HAD TOO MUCH TO DRINK TO DRIVE HOME. SOMETIMES WE KISS. SOMETIMES WE HAVE SEX. SOMETIMES IN THE MORNING I DO NOT REMEMBER THAT SHE IS THERE. SOMETIMES IN THE MORNING SHE DOES NOT REMEMBER HOW SHE GOT THERE. AND THIS DOES NOT HURT.

FLESH FILLS UP THE EMPTY SPACE THAT HURTS UNTIL I WAKE UP BY MYSELF AGAIN.

I COUNT THE DAYS UNTIL JET GETS BACK. PART OF ME HOPES SHE NEVER DOES.

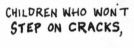

'IF YOU WERE TO ASK ME, I WOULD NEVER SAY I AM SUPERSTITIOUS.

I HAVE ALWAYS HATED THAT WORD, WHICH CONJURES UP...

WHAT?

CHILDREN WHO WON'T STEP ON CRACKS,

MEN WHO WON'T WALK UNDER LADDERS

AND WOMEN WHO SPIT ON THEIR FINGERS AND RUB THEIR EARS TO MAKE THE PEOPLE WHO ARE TALKING ABOUT THEM BITE THEIR TONGUES

I AM DRIVING WITH SETH, AND WHEN WE PASS UNDER YELLOW TRAFFIC LIGHTS, HE SCRAPES THE CAR CEILING TWICE WITH HIS FINGERS.

SKRITCH SKRITCH

WHY DO YOU DO THAT?

FOR GOOD LUCK!

WHEN I ASK HIM IF IT WORKS, HE SHRUGS.

WHEN WE PASS UNDER THE NEXT YELLOW LIGHT, I FEEL THE RASP OF THE CAR CEILING AGAINST MY FINGERS.

SKREEEE

I WEAR THE SAME SPECIAL NECKLACE WHEN I TAKE TESTS, DRIVE LONG DISTANCES, OR NEED SPECIAL ASSISTANCE.

I DO NOT **NEED** THIS NECKLACE, BUT I HAVE NEVER FAILED A TEST OR GOTTEN IN AN ACCIDENT WHILE WEARING IT.

WHEN I OPEN A NEW PACK OF CIGARETTES, I TURN THE FIRST ONE OVER.

EMPHA ZEE Lights

I AM DRIVING WITH DELIA, AND WHEN WE CROSS OVER RAILROAD TRACKS, SHE LIFTS HER FEET FROM THE CAR FLOOR.

WHY DO YOU DO THAT?

IT'S FOR GOOD LUCK

CERTAIN DEATH WHEN FLASHING

WHEN I ASK HER IF THIS WORKS, SHE SHRUGS.

WHEN WE NEXT CROSS RAILROAD TRACKS, I FEEL MY KNEES HIT THE BOTTOM OF THE DASH.

TUMP BOMP

I AM NOT SUPERSTITIOUS, BUT I DO NOT BELIEVE IN TEMPTING FATE, EITHER.

Another Joke I know

Captain Wilson is known far and wide for his excellent reputation. He has led his ship time and time again through seemingly insurmountable perils. It is a beautiful day when First Mate Perkins runs to him, terrified.

"Sir! There are three French vessels to port prepared to attack!"

Captain Wilson thrusts his noble chin forward. "Perkins! Ready the crew, and bring me my red cape!"

The battle is fought, Captain Wilson's ship emerging victorious.

It is the next day and First Mate Perkins runs to the captain, terrified. "Sir! There are four Italian vessels to starboard prepared to attack!"

Captain Wilson thrusts out his noble chin. "Perkins! Ready the crew, and bring me my red cape!"

The battle is fought, Captain Wilson's ship again emerging victorious.

The following day, First Mate Perkins runs again to the Captain, terrified.

"Sir! There are five Russian vessels dead ahead prepared to attack!"

Captain Wilson thrusts his noble chin forward. "Perkins! Ready the crew, and bring me my red cape!"

The battle is fought, Captain Wilson's ship again emerging victorious. After the battle, Perkins congratulates Captain Wilson on a battle well fought, and asks permission to ask a question.

"Of course, Perkins."

"Sir, I understand why you ask me to ready the crew before each battle, but why do you always ask me for your red cape as well?"

"Because, Perkins, if I am struck during battle and begin to bleed, it will match my red cape. The crew will not lose heart or fear for my sake, but will fight their best."

It is the fourth day, pouring rain and rough seas. First Mate Perkins runs to Captain Wilson, frightened to tears.

"Sir! There are three French vessels to port, four Italian vessels to starboard, and five Russian vessels straight ahead, all prepared to attack!"

"Perkins! Ready the crew and bring me my brown pants!"

NESTLED IN THE V OF HIS TEE-SHIRT, MY FATHER'S GREY CHEST HAIRS EMBRACE A BUDDHA HE AND MY MOTHER BOUGHT ON VACATION IN HAWAII THREE YEARS AGO, A SMALL STAR OF DAVID, AND A SAINT CHRISTOPEER MEDALLION HIS DOCTOR HAS GIVEN HIM. ONE DAY HE SLIPS THESE INTO THE DRAWER NEXT TO HIS BED.

WE DO NOT DISCUSS THIS.

MY LETTERS TO FRIENDS, FULL OF MASSIVE GRIPES, DO NOT ALWAYS REFLECT REALITY. I ALWAYS RESPOND TO "HOW ARE THINGS?" BY SAYING "ADEQUATE." I WAS FIVE WHEN MY GRANDMOTHER TOLD ME WHAT HER MOTHER TOLD HER, WHICH WAS WHAT HER MOTHER, TOO, TOLD HER:

TO SPEAK OF SUCCESS AND SATISFACTION IS TO PROVOKE DIRE MISFORTUNE

MY FATHER SITS FOR HOURS AT THE KITCHEN TABLE. HIS FACE IS HARD WITH CONCENTRATION. SOMETIMES HIS MOUTH SMILES, SOMETIMES IT CONTORTS IN ANGER AND FEAR. THE GAME IS SIMPLE. IF HE WINS, HE LIVES.

My great-uncle Oscar comes to live with us after his stroke and each time we part company we kiss his cheek and say "So long for now." Each night when we go to bed we say "Good night" and "Goodbye" are forbidden. "I'll see you in the morning."

In these ways we protect ourselves from CHAOS, reclaim our lives from FEAR, strive against the PARALYSIS OF HAPPENSTANCE.

MY FATHER HAS BEEN DEAD FORTY-FIVE MINUTES.

HIS DOCTOR HAS CLOSED HIS EYES AND WE ARE SITTING IN THE KITCHEN, WAITING FOR THE MEN TO TAKE HIS BODY AWAY. WHEN THEY ARRIVE, MY MOTHER RUNS INTO THE BEDROOM AND PLACES A SCRAP OF PAPER IN HIS HAND. IT IS YELLOW AND HEART-SHAPED, FROM THE TELEPHONE MESSAGE PAD. IT HAS OUR NAMES AND PHONE NUMBER ON IT. "SO THAT HE WILL BE ABLE TO FIND US LATER," SHE EXPLAINS. "HE MADE ME PROMISE." HER LIPS ARE PRESSED TIGHT, QUIVERING, AS SHE WIPES HER EYES AND POURS A DRINK.

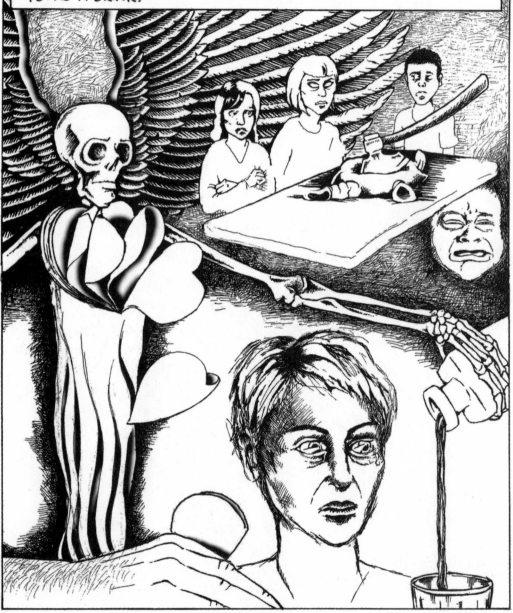

96

LOVE and LOSS

IT IS MY LAST DAY OF WORK, OR, MORE ACCURATELY, MY LAST MORNING. I HAVE BEEN WORKING ONLY PART-TIME THIS WEEK, SO THAT I CAN START PACKING THINGS UP IN THE APARTMENT, SHOP FOR SCHOOL SUPPLIES, BEGIN TO TIE UP LOOSE ENDS.

DOWN IN THE OFFICE, THERE IS A SUITCASE UNDER MY DESK. IN TWO HOURS, I LEAVE TO GO TO FLORIDA, TO ATTEND MAISIE AND DOUG'S WEDDING, WHICH THEY HAVE DECIDED TO HOLD EVEN THOUGH SHE HAS MISCARRIED. THE GUESTS HAVE ALREADY BEEN INVITED.

I AM NOT THINKING ABOUT HOW MUCH I HATE CEREMONIES WHICH BEGIN AND END THE SAME WAY FOR EVERYONE, AND I AM NOT WONDERING WHO WILL GIVE THE FATHERLESS MAISIE AWAY AT THE WEDDING.

I AM TRYING TO TIE UP LOOSE ENDS AT WORK, GET THE LAST FEW SIGNATURES BEFORE TIME RUNS OUT. THIS IS THE LAST CHANCE I HAVE TO FIND OUT IF THE VITULLO CHILD HAS REGAINED CONSCIOUSNESS, IF CLEOPATRA CLAYMORE IS SOBER ENOUGH TO SIGN HER NAME, WHOSE CAR IT WAS THAT KIM NORWICH WAS IN WHEN IT CRASHED.

NO GUARDIAN IS PRESENT FOR THE VITULLO CHILD, CLEOPATRA IS ASLEEP, AND KIM HAS BEEN WHEELED AWAY TO PHYSICAL THERAPY, AND SO THERE ARE NO GRATIFYING CONCLUSIONS. IN KIM'S ROOM, THERE IS AN ELDERLY WOMAN WITH HAIR LIKE SO MANY COBWEBS TANGLED AROUND HER HEAD. THE TWO ORDERLIES WHO PIN HER DOWN TO HER BED TAKE NO NOTICE OF ME.

NOW, ALICE, DON'T YOU WANT TO GET BETTER?

PLEASE, ALICE, ALL WE NEED IS A LITTLE BIT OF YOUR BLOOD

MAMA, PLEASE. BE GOOD DON'T MAKE A FUSS.

NO.

CALM DOWN, ALICE. WHY CAN'T WE HAVE YOUR BLOOD? IT WON'T HURT.

NO NO NO NO YOU CAN'T HAVE MY BLOOD!

I PUT THE ENVELOPE WITH THE INSURANCE ASSIGNMENT BY THE MIRROR, AND START OUT THE DOOR.
"YOU CAN'T HAVE MY BLOOD. YOU DON'T LOVE ME." I RETURN TO THE OFFICE SIGNATURELESS, HAPPILY RESIGNED TO USE PAPERWORK TO FILL THE FORTY-FIVE MINUTES BEFORE LOGAN PICKS ME UP.

INSTEAD, THERE IS A PIZZA ON MY DESK, AND A LITER OF COLA, AND A CAKE, AND A GIFT. JUDY, MELANIE, AND LOUISE SMILE BROADLY.

SUHPRISE!!

°°NO!

ROTTO BROWN

UNCOMFORTABLE AND ALWAYS BAD AT GOODBYES, I SMILE SHEEPISHLY, AND WE EAT PIZZA AND DRINK COLA. WHEN WE ARE FINISHED, I OPEN THE PRESENT, SMILE AT THE STUFFED BEAR DRESSED AS A DOCTOR, READ THE CARD SIGNED BY PEOPLE AT THE OTHER OFFICE WHO I NEVER MET. WE HUG WHEN LOGAN APPEARS, AND THEN I LEAVE, MY I.D. CARD FACE DOWN ON THE EMPTY DESK.

LOGAN AND I KISS AT THE AIRPORT.
"SEE YOU WHEN YOU GET BACK, RIGHT?" HE ASKS.

"YUP."
WE DO NOT SAY GOODBYE.

JOKES AND the UN-CONSCIENCE

I HAVE ALWAYS HATED THE DRESS MY MOTHER GAVE ME FOR MY TWENTIETH BIRTHDAY. IT NEVER FIT QUITE RIGHT, AND SO I AM WEARING IT TODAY, A HATED DRESS FOR A HATED OCCASION.

MY BROTHER SITS NEXT TO ME, HIS NEW JACKET SOFT BLACK AGAINST SLICK BURGUNDY INTERIOR.

IN MAY, MY FATHER SAID, "JUSTIN, YOU MUST GO AND BUY A JACKET TODAY. YOU WILL NOT HAVE TIME TO GET ONE WHEN YOU NEED IT. SASHA, DO YOU HAVE SHOES?"

THERE WAS NO JOY IN OUR PURCHASES. WE MODELED THEM, DREADING THE INEVITABLE TIME WHEN WE WOULD NEXT WEAR THEM.

WE HAVE NEVER BEEN IN A LIMOUSINE BEFORE, AND SO JUSTIN AND I OPEN EVERY COMPARTMENT, FIND THE TELEVISION AND THE VCR, THE UNSTOCKED BAR, GIGGLING AT OUR NEW TOY.

PUT THAT CIGARETTE OUT, SASHA. THE SMOKE IS MAKING ME SICK.

MY MOTHER IS HEADACHY, HUNG-OVER FROM TOO MUCH OF MY UNCLE'S SYMPATHY AND SCOTCH.

NO ONE TALKS ON THE RIDE TO THE CEMETERY. THE DRIVER HUMS SOFTLY TO HIMSELF, IN TIME WITH THE SLAP-SLAP OF THE WINDSHIELD WIPERS.

IT IS TOO RAINY AND DARK FOR EARLY JUNE

EVERYONE ELSE HAS A LITTLE PIECE OF RIPPED BLACK RIBBON PINNED TO THEIR CLOTHES. I HAVE LOST TWO ALREADY, AND AM NOT EAGER TO ASK THE RABBI FOR A THIRD.

THEY HAVE A MIND OF THEIR OWN AND REFUSE TO STAY WITH ME.

THE WET OF THE GRASS SOAKS MY SHOES IMMEDIATELY. I LOOK SOMEWHERE OUT IN SPACE AS ALL THE RELATIVES I HAVE NEVER MET KISS MY CHEEK, PAT MY BACK, TELL ME WHAT A PLEASURE IT IS TO MEET ME, "THOUGH, DEAR, I WISH WE COULD HAVE DONE THIS UNDER BETTER CIRCUMSTANCES — WHY WEREN'T YOU AT THE REUNION?"

I HATE ALL OF THEM TODAY, WITH THEIR NEW YORK ACCENTS, THE MEN WITH THEIR SKINNY MUSTACHES AND GOLD CHAINS AND RINGS, THE WOMEN WITH TOO MUCH PERFUME AND PLASTIC FLOWERED RAIN HATS PROTECTING FRESH-FROM-THE-PARLOR HAIRSTYLES. I HATE MY GRANDFATHER WHO BURSTS INTO TEARS AS SOON AS WE GET TO THE GRAVESITE. HE IS CONFUSED, BALD AND BLUBBERING, HE THINKS HE IS HERE FOR MY GRANDMOTHER'S FUNERAL A FEW MONTHS EARLIER.

MY AUNT GUIDES HIM BACK FROM THE GRAVESITE, WHERE HE HAS RUN WITH OUTSTRETCHED ARMS, CALLING, "REBECCA!" SHE WALKS HIM TO A CHAIR, KEEPS HIM THERE WITH WITH THE PALM OF HER HAND ON HIS HEAD. THE ANGER IS RISING INSIDE ME AS HE SOBS INTO HIS HANDS, "OH, HE'S WHERE HE BELONGS, BACK WITH HIS MOMMA. SHE NEVER SAW ENOUGH OF HIM, AND NOW SHE'S GOT HER BOY WITH HER, AT HER FEET. REBECCA!"

THE UMBRELLAS ABOVE OUR HEADS LIKE CHEAP PLASTIC FLOWERS.

UNDER A PLASTIC TARP IS THE CASKET, WHICH MY MOTHER AND SISTER SHOPPED FOR, MY SISTER INFURIATED BY MARTY THE MORTICIAN, WHO TRIED TO HUG HER.

HE POINTED TO ONE CASKET, TAPPED IT AFFECTIONATELY, AND SAID, "THIS IS WHAT I BURIED MY PARENTS IN, BUT," TAPPING ANOTHER, "THIS IS THE ONE I WANT. REAL MAHOGANY. FIVE THOUSAND DOLLARS."

LOOK! $999

ALL ALONG, THE REMINDER THAT THIS FUNERAL IS NOT FOR US, BUT FOR MY FATHER'S FATHER AND SISTER. THIS IS WHY WE COULD NOT HAVE THE SIMPLE PINE BOX, PROUD IN ITS SIMPLICITY, IN ITS HON-ESTY.

INSTEAD, MY FATHER IS INSIDE SOMETHING THAT LOOKS LIKE A TACKY LEAD WEDDING CAKE.

("SASHA, TRY AND BE MORE UNDERSTANDING. THE MOST HORRIBLE THING FOR ANYONE IS TO HAVE TO BURY THEIR CHILDREN.")

I AM TRYING TO BE MORE UNDERSTANDING. ONE FAMILIAR FACE, A FAMILY FRIEND, GRABS MY HAND, WHISPERS IN MY EAR, "YOUR FATHER WOULD'VE HATED THIS. KEEP IN MIND, HE WOULDN'T BE HERE IF HE'D HAD THE CHOICE."

I LAUGH AND IT COMES TOO LOUD, TOO HARD FOR A CEMETARY, AN ALIVE SOUND.

FOR A SECOND, I AM NOT ANGRY, JUST EMBARRASSED, COVERING MY MOUTH.

AND THEN THE RABBI BEGINS TO SPEAK. HE IS FAT. HE HAS CURLY HAIR. THE YARMULKA IS PREPOSTEROUSLY TINY ON HIS INFLATED HEAD. I HATE HIM, TOO.

"GOOD AFTERNOON," HE BEGINS. I DO NOT KNOW WHAT TO DO WITH THE RIDICULOUSNESS OF THIS SITUATION. I AM AT A FUNERAL FOR MY FATHER, SURROUNDED BY FAMILY MEMBERS I KNOW HE HATED, TO WHOM HE NEVER TALKED. I AM LISTENING TO A RABBI HE'D NEVER MET SUMMARIZE HIS LIFE, TRY AND REDUCE IT TO A MORAL.

THE INJUSTICE OF THE CEREMONY, THE PRAYER WHICH IS THE SAME FOR EVERYONE.

IT GETS WORSE FROM HERE.

THE RABBI USES MY MOTHER'S MIDDLE NAME INSTEAD OF HER GIVEN NAME, BECAUSE HE DOES NOT KNOW THE DIFFERENCE. HE CONFUSES ALL THE FAMILY STORIES TOLD TO HIM THE NIGHT BEFORE, INTEGRATES THEM LIKE TWENTY-FIVE JOKES REASSEMBLED WITH THE WRONG PUNCHLINES.

A COMMENT MY SENILE, GRIEF-STRICKEN GRANDFATHER MADE, "WE NEVER GOT TO SEE HIM," COMES SAILING FROM THE RABBI AS

ALAN WAS A MAN DEVOTED FIRST AND FOREMOST TO HIS CAREER, AND THEREFORE WAS NOT ABLE TO SEE MUCH OF HIS FAMILY.

THOUGH HE WAS NOT AROUND TO WITNESS THE CHILDREN GROWING UP, HE LOVED THEM TERRIBLY...

I AM WONDERING IF I AM AT THE RIGHT FUNERAL. I SEE MY AUNT SARA'S FACE, CONTORTED WITH PAIN, SEE MY MOTHER STOIC, AND MY GRANDFATHER MESSILY WAILING INTO A HANDKERCHIEF PROCURED FOR HIM BY MARTY THE MORTICIAN.

THIS MUST BE THE PLACE.

THE RABBI GETS ONE STORY MORE OR LESS RIGHT.

"HIS WIFE RELATED A STORY WHICH I WOULD LIKE TO REPEAT. ALAN WAS AN AVID SKIER, AS IS THE ENTIRE FAMILY. THEY WERE ON VACATION OUT WEST AND HAD BEEN SKIING ALL DAY. SASHA, DEIDRE AND JUSTIN WERE TIRED AND WANTED TO GO IN.

WELL, ALAN LOOKED AT THEM AND SAID, 'COME ON, JUST ONE MORE.' THE CHILDREN WERE TOO TIRED, BUT HE AND MARY WENT UP AND 'ROCKED ON DOWN THAT SLOPE,' TO USE HER WORDS, JUST ONE MORE TIME. WELL, I THINK THAT ALAN IS A MAN WHO WOULD WANT US TO SAY OF HIM,

'FORGET THAT I DIED-'"

THE RABBI GETS ONE STORY MORE OR LESS RIGHT, BUT BENDS IT INTO CHEESY FUNERAL SPEAK. HE'S TURNED A PLEASANT MEMORY INTO A SUNSET FOR MY FATHER TO RIDE INTO. THERE IS NO MENTION OF THE ICE PACKS ON HIS SWOLLEN KNEES AFTERWARD, OR OF HOW HE HAD TO BE HELPED DOWN THE STAIRS FOR A DAY.

THERE IS NO MENTION OF HOW HE YELLED AT THE THREE OF US FOR SKIING TOO FAST. OR HOW HE RAGED AT MY BROTHER FOR NOT WANTING TO SKI BECAUSE HE WAS ACTITUDE SICK. --

THE RELATIVES NOD SAGELY. OH YES, THEY'RE THINKING TO THEMSELVES. THAT'S THE MAN I KNEW, ROCKING DOWN THOSE SLOPES.

"FORGET THAT I DIED - REMEMBER THAT I LIVED"

THE RABBI OPENS HIS MOUTH - HE IS SINGING HEBREW AND HE HAS A LOVELY VOICE.

NO ONE HAS PREPARED ME FOR THIS.

I HAVE NEVER BEEN TO A FUNERAL BEFORE AND OF COURSE THERE ARE NO FUNERAL REHEARSALS THE WAY THERE ARE WEDDING REHEARSALS.

I SHOULD BE THINKING OF MY FATHER, COMMENDING HIS SOUL, BUT THERE IS A FAT MAN IN A TINY HAT IN FRONT OF ME SINGING.

I REALIZE THAT I AM GOING TO LAUGH. I CAN'T LAUGH AT MY FATHER'S FUNERAL.

WHAT GREATER INSULT COULD THERE POSSIBLY BE? I CAN'T LAUGH.

I CAN'T HELP IT.

I COVER MY FACE AND START TO CHOKE, TRYING TO REIN IT TIGHT IN-SIDE. CHOKING IS ACCEPTABLE.

I AM BRIGHT RED TRYING TO CATCH MY BREATH. I LOOK UP, MY MOTHER'S CONCERNED FACE GAZING AT ME. SHE THINKS I HAVE BEEN SOBBING.

I LOOK AT MY BROTHER. JUSTIN'S MOUTH IS AS CONTORTED AS MINE IS—HE LEANS TOWARD ME AND WHISPERS IN MY EAR,

DO YOU THINK HE KNOWS "MELANCHOLY BABY"?

AND IT IS ALL OVER, I AM CHOKING AGAIN, TURNING BRIGHT RED AGAIN. MY BROTHER IS NOT AS PROFICIENT AT SUPRESSING HIS GIGGLES. RELATIVES LOOK OVER.

WE ARE MAKING NOISE.

HELPLESS, I LOOK AT MY MOTHER. SHE IS STERN, AND SHE AND DEIRDRE SILENCE US WITH LOOKS.

WE HAVE FORGOTTEN WHERE WE ARE

AS QUICKLY AS THE LAUGHTER CAME, IT IS GONE, AND THE PLACE WHERE IT CAME FROM IS HURTING AND SORE.

THERE IS A PAUSE. LITTLE CARDS ARE BEING PASSED OUT AMONG US, WITH HEBREW ON ONE SIDE, PHONETIC ENGLISH ON THE OTHER. I REALIZE I CAN REDEEM MY-SELF. I WILL READ THE FINAL PRAYER IN HEBREW.

FOR MY FATHER.

HE WILL HEAR ME AND UNDERSTAND, FORGIVE MY LAUGHTER.

WITH EVERYONE ELSE, I START READING.

BUT I AM ALREADY TWO SYLLABLES BEHIND BY THIRD WORD, FRUSTRATED AND CLOSE TO TEARS. MY MOUTH MOVES IN ALL THE WRONG WAYS.

I LOOK OVER, NEXT TO ME, AND DEIRDRE AND JUSTIN HAVE COVERED THEIR FACES. THEY ARE SHAKING VIOLENTLY, TRYING NOT TO LAUGH AT ME. JUSTIN IS LAUGHING SO HARD HE'S RETCHING. I GIVE UP AND COUGH AND CHOKE BEHIND MY HANDS.

WHEN I CAN BREATHE NORMALLY AGAIN, IT IS ALL OVER. A FEW UMBRELLAS SAIL TOWARDS THE PARKING LOT. A FEW RELATIVES TALK AMONGST THEM-SELVES ABOUT WHO WILL PICK UP THE FRUIT AND CHEESE PLATTERS FROM THE DELI FOR THE RECEPTION AT MY AUNT'S.

NO ONE ELSE IS WATCHING THE FOUR MEN IN OVERALLS WHO HAVE COME WITH SHOVELS. THEY BEGIN TO FILL IN THE HOLE.

DIRT AND ROCKS HIT THE STEEL WEDDING CAKE.

FOUR MEN WITH SHOVELS AND THEY ARE PUTTING DIRT ON MY FATHER'S COFFIN AND SUDDENLY I AM CRYING, MAKING MORE NOISE THAN MY GRAND-FATHER.

THERE IS A HAND ON MY SHOULDER. IT IS THE RABBI'S. I WANT TO SHOVE HIM AWAY, BUT I DO NOT. HE LEADS ME BACK TO THE LIMOUSINE.

I TAKE ONE LAST LOOK OVER MY SHOULDER AND UNDER MY BREATH I WHISPER "GOODBYE."

ANOTHER JOKE I KNOW

A grieving woman goes to the funeral parlor to make arrangements for her husband's burial.

"As you can see," she says, "he died wearing his brown suit. However, he has to be buried wearing a black suit."

The funeral director is puzzled.

"Can't we just bury him in the brown suit?" he asks the woman. "It's a perfectly nice suit."

"No," she says. "It has to be black." The mortician assures her that he will take care of matters and her husband will be buried in a black suit, and the widow hands him a blank check to cover the cost.

At the open-casket viewing, the widow is delighted to see her husband in an extremely expensive, new black suit. "It's perfect!" she cries. "How much was it?" "Well," says the director, "It didn't cost a thing. Right after you left, a man was brought in wearing a black suit who was about the same size. I asked his wife if she minded burying him in a brown suit instead, and she said it was fine. So I switched the heads."

JOLLY TIME

DISTANCE

Every time I'm on a plane, I'm amazed that these big, heavy things can stay in the air - how we can be held high above the earth's surface and then brought down intact; that these metal monsters can defy logic and soar; that we can defy gravity and survive. Within some parameters, every plane ride is familiar once you've done it: the size of the seats, the tiny overhead screens, the small blankets, the sanitary and almost inedible food, the carpeted walkway on either side of the flight, the flight attendants' spiel. The best flights are almost completely forget-table while the reasons for travel seldom are: vacations, wed-dings, births, funerals. In between, up high in the air, there is distance, there is time; the distance between places, the time between events. Up high over America, my head is trying to get perspective on my summer, all the people in all the rooms in the hospital giving birth or getting better or dying; my dad's illness and death and funeral; Maisie's wedding and love and love?; the upcoming fall school semester; the rest of my life. It's hard to know where to go from here, what's next, when the ache will go, what it feels like to live without a father, what it feels like to live without the love of a father, what it feels like to live without the fear of a father, how to go on, how to go forward, how to soar when you're a tons-heavy monster. I'm finding out, minute by minute.

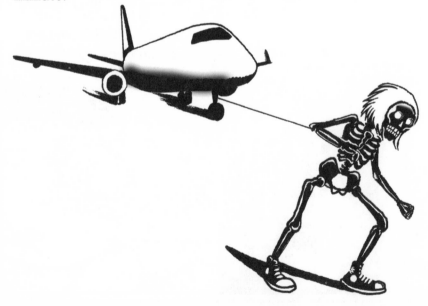

This is what it feels like to put the seat back into an upright position without a father, I think to myself.

This is what it feels like to walk down the carpeted jetway without a father.

This is what it feels like to walk through the airport without a father.

THE FEELING I GET WHEN I SEE JET WALKING TOWARDS ME AT THE BAGGAGE CLAIM, HOWEVER, HAS ABSOLUTELY NOTHING TO DO WITH MY FATHER.

I DON'T KNOW WHAT IT MEANS ABOUT THE REST OF MY LIFE, HOW TO GO FORWARD FROM HERE, BUT IT'S EVERYTHING I WANT.

YOU READY?

YOU GOT EVERYTHING? LET'S GO.

LAUGHING STOCK

I know a lot of jokes.
I know jokes about ship captains,
doctors and morticians.
I know jokes about jokes.

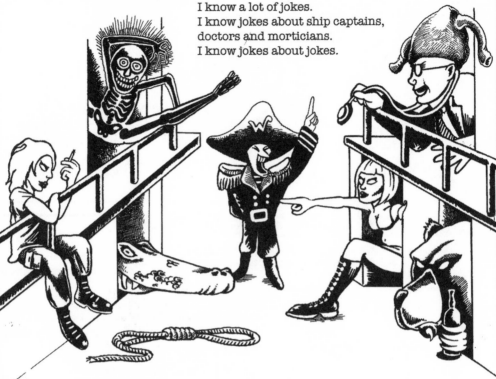

There is one that takes place in a prison and has the inmates
calling out numbers to each other. Fred yells out "Twenty-three!"
and laughter rocks the prison. Joel yells "Thirty-five!" and a peal
of laughter follows. The new inmate turns to his cellmate, Monty,
and asks him what is going on. Monty explains that they've all
been there for so long, that there is no longer any point in the
retelling jokes in their entirety anymore. They have given each
joke a number, and they simply call the number.
"Go ahead and try it," Monty urges the new inmate. The new inmate rubs his hands together and eagerly calls out -

TWENTY-ONE!

The prison is quiet. Monty shrugs,
and tells the new inmate -

SOME PEOPLE CAN TELL A JOKE,
AND SOME PEOPLE CAN'T.

I know jokes about women. I know jokes about men.
I know jokes about cats, dogs, about rabbits and re-
frigerators, bears and barbiturates.
I know a lot of jokes about people in bars.

There is a joke and it is about lament and laughter,
fear and forgetting. It is a very warm thing, this joke,
and when I learn it, this is where it will go.

You ready?
You got everything?
Let's go.

About the Author

San Francisco–based performance poet Daphne Gottlieb stitches together the ivory tower and the gutter just using her tongue. She is the editor of *Homewrecker: An Adultery Reader* (Soft Skull Press), as well as the author of *Final Girl* (Soft Skull Press), *Why Things Burn* (Soft Skull Press) and *Pelt* (Odd Girls Press). She is currently at work on her next book of poetry, *Kissing Dead Girls*.

About the Artist

Diane DiMassa is the author of *The Complete Hothead Paisan: Homicidal Lesbian Terrorist* (Cleis Press). She has contributed to many anthologies and shown her work in group and solo shows. This is her first graphic novel. DiMassa lives in Bridgeport, Connecticut.